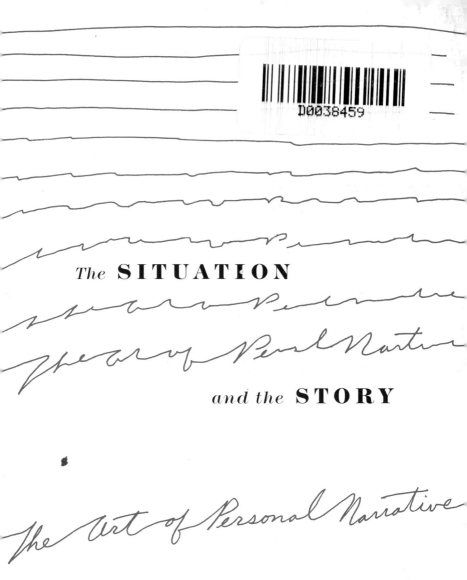

The SITUATION

and the STORY

The Art of Personal Narrative

VIVIAN GORNICK

NEW EDITION FOR WRITERS, TEACHERS, AND STUDENTS

Praise from writers and teachers for
The Situation and the Story

"A wonderful illumination of some of the best and most moving writers of personal narrative, by a writer whose own graceful style and exemplary forthrightness make this a most rewarding book for both the classroom and one's own favorite armchair."

—Lydia Davis, State University of New York, Albany, author of *Samuel Johnson Is Indignant*

"We have long needed a book like this, which would put the field of creative nonfiction into thoughtful perspective, X-ray its secrets, and raise its standards. Vivian Gornick has done all that and more, producing a brilliant exegesis that is both analysis and exemplar of the difficult art of personal narrative. She brings a laser-like focus to her subject, while complicating it at every turn with moral nuance. The writing is both eloquent and elegant; the sentences have bite; the whole thing is an exhilarating read."

—Phillip Lopate, Hofstra University, author of *Portrait of My Body*

"I loved *The Situation and the Story*. It has changed my thinking already and should be on every writer's bookshelf."

—Elaine Showalter, Princeton University, author of *A Literature of Their Own*

VIVIAN GORNICK

The Situation and the Story

Vivian Gornick's books include *Fierce Attachments*, *Approaching Eye Level*, and *The End of the Novel of Love*, which was a finalist for the National Book Critics Circle Award in 1998. She lives in New York City.

The SITUATION
and the STORY

The SITUATION
and the STORY

The Art of Personal Narrative

New Edition for

Writers, Teachers, and Students

VIVIAN GORNICK

Farrar, Straus and Giroux

New York

Farrar, Straus and Giroux
19 Union Square West, New York 10003

Distributed in Canada by Douglas & McIntyre Ltd.
Printed in the United States of America
Published in 2001 by Farrar, Straus and Giroux
First paperback edition, 2002

Owing to limitations of space, all acknowledgments for permission to
reprint previously published material can be found on page 175.

Library of Congress Cataloging-in-Publication Data
Gornick, Vivian.
    The situation and the story : the art of personal narrative / Vivian
Gornick— New ed. for writers, teachers, and students, 1st pbk. ed.
        p.   cm.
    Includes bibliographical references.
    ISBN 0-374-52858-6 (pbk. : alk. paper)
    1. Autobiography. 2. English prose literature—History and
criticism. 3. American prose literature—History and criticism.
4. English language—Rhetoric. 5. Autobiography—Authorship.
6. Narration (Rhetoric) I. Title.

PR756.A9 G67 2002
820.9'492—dc21

                                                         2002026415

Designed by Lisa Stokes

www.fsgbooks.com

10   9   8   7   6   5   4

The SITUATION and the STORY

A pioneering doctor died and a large number
of people spoke at her memorial service. Repeatedly it was said by colleagues, patients, activists in health
care reform that the doctor had been tough, humane, brilliant; stimulating and dominant; a stern teacher, a dyna-
mite researcher, an astonishing listener. I sat among the
silent mourners. Each speaker provoked in me a measure
of thoughtfulness, sentiment, even regret, but only one
among them—a doctor in her forties who had been
trained by the dead woman—moved me to that melancholy evocation of world-and-self that makes a single person's death feel large. The speaker had not known the
dead doctor any better or more intimately than the others;
nor had she anything new to add to the collective portrait

we had already been given. Yet *her* words had deepened the atmosphere and penetrated my heart. Why? I wondered, even as I brushed away the tears. Why had *these* words made a difference?

The question must have lingered in me because the next morning I awakened to find myself sitting bolt upright in bed, the eulogy standing in the air before me like a composition. That was it, I realized. It had been composed. That is what had made the difference.

The eulogist had been remembering herself as a young doctor coming under the formative influence of the older one. The memory had acted as an organizing principle that determined the structure of her remarks. Structure had imposed order. Order made the sentences more shapely. Shapeliness increased the expressiveness of the language. Expressiveness deepened association. At last, a dramatic buildup occurred, one that had layered into it the descriptive feel of a young person's apprenticeship, medical practices in a time of social change, and a divided attachment to a mentor who could bring herself only to correct, never to praise. This buildup is called texture. It was the texture that had stirred me; caused me to feel, with powerful immediacy, not only the actuality of the woman being remembered but—even more vividly—the presence of the one doing the remembering. The speaker's effort to recall with exactness how things had been between herself and the dead woman—her open need to make sense of a strong but vexing relationship—had caused her to say so much that I became aware at last of all that was *not* being said; that which could never be said. I felt acutely the warm, painful inadequacy of human relations. This feeling resonated in me. It was the resonance that had lingered on, exactly as it does when the last page is turned of a book that reaches the heart.

The more I thought about the achieved quality of the eulogy, the more clearly I saw how central the eulogist herself had been to its effectiveness. The speaker had "composed" her thoughts the better to recall the apprentice she had once been, the one formed by that strong but vexing relationship. As she spoke, we could see her in her mentor's presence, sharply alive to the manner and appearance of a teacher at once profoundly intelligent and profoundly cutting. There she was, now eager, now flinching, now dug in. It was the act of imagining herself as she had once been that enriched her syntax and extended not only her images but the coherent flow of association that led directly into the task at hand.

The better the speaker imagined herself, the more vividly she brought the dead doctor to life. It was, after all, a baptism by fire that was being described. To see her ambitious young self burning to know what her mentor knew, we had to see the mentor as well: an agent of threat and promise: a figure of equal complexity. The volatility of their exchange brought us to the heart of the reminiscence. The older doctor had been as embroiled as the younger one in a struggle of will and temperament that had joined them at the hip. The story here was not either the speaker or the doctor per se; it was what happened to each of them in the other's company. The place in which they met as talented belligerents was the one the eulogist had her eye on. It was *here* that she had engaged. This was what had supplied her her balanced center.

It was remarkable to me how excellent were relations between this narrator and this narration. The speaker never lost sight of why she was speaking—or, perhaps more important, of *who* was speaking. Of the various selves at her disposal (she was, after all, many people—a daughter, a lover, a bird-watcher, a New Yorker), she knew and didn't forget that the only proper self to invoke was the one that had been apprenticed. That was the self in whom this story resided. A self—now here was a curiosity—that never lost interest in its own animated existence at the same time that it lived only to eulogize the dead doctor. This last, I thought, was crucial: the element most responsible for the striking clarity of intent the eulogy had demonstrated. Because the narrator knew *who* was speaking, she always knew *why* she was speaking.

■   ■   ■

The writing we call personal narrative is written by people who, in essence, are imagining only themselves: in relation to the subject in hand. The connection is an intimate one; in fact, it is critical. Out of the raw material of a writer's own undisguised being a narrator is fashioned whose existence on the page is integral to the tale being told. This narrator becomes a persona. Its tone of voice, its angle of vision, the rhythm of its sentences, what it selects to observe and what to ignore are chosen to serve the subject; yet at the same time the way the narrator—or the persona—sees things is, to the largest degree, the thing being seen.

To fashion a persona out of one's own undisguised self is no easy thing. A novel or a poem provides invented characters or speaking voices that act as surrogates for the writer. Into those surrogates will be poured all that the writer cannot address directly—inappropriate longings, defensive embarrassments, anti-social desires—but must address to achieve felt reality. The persona in a nonfiction narrative is an unsurrogated one. Here the writer must identify openly with those very same defenses and embarrassments that the novelist or the poet is once removed from. It's like lying down on the couch in public—and while a writer may be willing to do just that, it is a strategy that most often simply doesn't work. Think of how many years on the couch it takes to speak about oneself, but without all the whining and complaining, the self-hatred and the self-justification that make the analysand a bore to all the world but the analyst. The unsurrogated narrator has the monumental task of transforming low-level self-interest into the kind of detached empathy required of a piece of writing that is to be of value to the disinterested reader.

Yet the creation of such a persona is vital in an essay or a memoir. It is the instrument of illumination. Without it there is neither subject nor story. To achieve it, the writer of memoir or essay undergoes an apprenticeship as soul-searching as any undergone by novelist or poet: the twin struggle to know not only why one is speaking but *who* is speaking.

The beauty of the eulogist's delivery had been the clarity of her intent. Working backward, we can figure out for ourselves how hard earned that clarity must have been. Invited to speak about an experience she had lived with for more than twenty years, the eulogist must have thought, A piece of cake, the story will write itself. Then she sat down to it, and very quickly discovered herself stymied. Well, what *about* the experience? What exactly was it? And where was it? The experience, it seemed, was a large piece of territory. How was she to enter it? From what angle, and in what position? With what strategy, and toward what end? The eulogist is flooded with confusion. She realizes suddenly that what she's been calling experience is only raw material.

Now she starts thinking. Who exactly *was* the doctor to her? Or she to the doctor? And what does it mean, having known her? What does she want this remembrance to exemplify? or embody? or invoke? What *is* it that she is really wanting to say? Questions not easy for a eulogist to ask much less answer, as many failed commemorations demonstrate, among them, famously, James Baldwin's of Richard Wright, in which a talented writer comes to honor his dead mentor and ends by trashing him because he can't figure out how to face his own mixed feelings.

Precisely the place to which our eulogist finally puzzles her way: her own mixed feelings. First she sees that she has them. Then she acknowledges them to herself. Then she considers them as a way into the experience. Then she realizes they *are* the experience. She begins to write.

Penetrating the familiar is by no means a given. On the contrary, it is hard, hard work.

◾ ◾ ◾

I began my own working life in the 1970s as a writer of what was then called personal journalism, a hybrid term meaning part personal essay, part social criticism. On the barricades for radical feminism, it had seemed natural to me from the minute I sat down at the typewriter to use myself—that is, to use my own response to a circumstance or an event—as a means of making some larger sense of things. At the time, of course, that was a shared instinct. Many other writers felt similarly compelled. The personal had become political, and the headlines metaphoric. We all felt implicated. We all felt that immediate experience signified. Wherever a writer looked, there was a narrative line to be drawn from the political tale being told on a march, at a party, during a chance encounter. Three who did it brilliantly during those years were Joan Didion, Tom Wolfe, and Norman Mailer.

From the beginning I saw the dangers of this kind of writing, saw what remarkable focus it would take to maintain the right balance between me and the story. Personal journalism had already thrown up many examples of people rushing into print with no clear idea of the relation between narrator and subject; writers were repeatedly falling into the pit of confessionalism or therapy on the page or naked self-absorption.

I don't know how well or how consistently I practiced what I had begun to preach to myself, but invariably I took it as my task to keep the narrating self subordinated to the idea in hand. I knew that I was never to tell an anecdote, fashion a description, indulge in a speculation whose point turned on me. I was to use myself only to clarify the argument, develop the analysis, push the story forward. I thought my grasp of the situation accurate and my self-consciousness sufficient. The reliable reporter in me would guarantee the trustworthy narrator.

One day a book editor approached me with an idea that struck a note of response. I had confided in her the tale of an intimate friendship I'd made with an Egyptian whose childhood in Cairo had strongly resembled my own in the Bronx. The resemblance had induced an ardent curiosity about "them"; and now I was being invited to go to Egypt, to write about middle-class Cairenes.

I said yes with easy pleasure, assuming that I would do in Cairo what I had been doing in New York. That is, I'd put myself down in the middle of the city, meet the people, turn them into encounters, use my own fears and prejudices to let them become themselves, and then I'd *make* something of it.

But Cairo was not New York, and personal journalism turned out not exactly the right job description.

The city was a bombardment of stimuli—dusty, crowded, noisy, alive and in pain—and the people—dark, nervous, intelligent; ignorant, volatile, needy; familiar, somehow very familiar—after all, how far from the idiom of excitable ghetto Jews was that of urban Muslims. The familiarity was my downfall. It excited and confused me. I fell in love with it and I romanticized it, made a mystery of the atmosphere and of myself in it. Who was I? Who were *they*? *Where* was I, and what was it all about? The problem was I didn't really want the answers to these questions. I found the "unknowingness" of things alluring. I thought it fine to lose myself in it. But when one makes a romance out of not knowing, the reliable reporter is in danger of becoming the untrustworthy narrator. And to a large degree she did.

I spent six hardworking months in Cairo. Morning, noon, and night I was out with Egyptians: doctors, housewives, journalists; students, lawyers, guides; friends, neighbors, lovers. It seemed to me that there was no more interesting thing in the world to do than to hang out with these people who smoked passionately, spoke with intensity, were easily agitated, and seemed consumed with a nervous tenderness applied to themselves and to one another. I thought their condition profound, and I identified with it. Instead of analyzing my subject, I merged with my subject. The Egyptians loved their own anxiety, thought it made them poetic. I got right into it, loving and dramatizing it as much as they did. Anecdote after anecdote collected in my notes, each one easily suffused with the fever of daily life in Cairo. Merely to reproduce it, I thought, would be to tell a story.

Such identification in writing has its uses and its difficulties, and in my book on Egypt the narration reflects both. On the one hand, the prose is an amazement of energy, crowded with description and response. On the other, the sentences are often rhetorical, the tone ejaculatory, the syntax overloaded. Where one adjective will do, three are sure to appear. Where quiet would be useful, agitation fills the page. Egypt was a country of indiscriminate expressiveness overflowing its own margins. My book does this curious thing: it mimics Egypt itself. That is its strength and its limitation.

It seemed to me for a long time that the problem had been detachment: I hadn't had any, hadn't even known it was a thing to be prized; that, in fact, without detachment there can be no story; description and response, yes, but no story. Even so, the confusion went deeper. When I had been a working journalist, politics had provided me with a situation, and polemics had given me my story. Now, in Egypt, I was in free fall, confused by a kind of writing whose requirements I did not understand but whose power I felt jerked around by. It wasn't personal journalism I was trying to write; it was personal narrative. It would be years before I sat down at the desk with sufficient command of the distinction to control the material. That is, to serve the situation and tell the kind of story I now wanted to tell.

■　　　■　　　■

Every work of literature has both a situation and a story. The situation is the context or circumstance, sometimes the plot; the story is the emotional experience that preoccupies the writer: the insight, the wisdom, the thing one has come to say. In *An American Tragedy* the situation is Dreiser's America; the story is the pathological nature of hunger for the world. In Edmund Gosse's memoir *Father and Son* the situation is fundamentalist England in the time of Darwin; the story is the betrayal of intimacy necessary to the act of becoming oneself. In a poem called "In the Waiting Room" Elizabeth Bishop describes herself at the age of seven, during the First World War, sitting in a dentist's office, turning the pages of *National Geographic*, listening to the muted cries of pain her timid aunt utters from within. That's the situation. The story is a child's first experience of isolation: her own, her aunt's, and that of the world.

Augustine's *Confessions* remains something of a model for the memoirist. In it, Augustine tells the tale of his conversion to Christianity. That's the situation. In this tale, he moves from an inchoate sense of being to a coherent sense of being, from an idling existence to a purposeful one, from a state of ignorance to one of truth. That's the story. Inevitably, it's a story of self-discovery and self-definition.

The subject of autobiography is always self-definition, but it cannot be self-definition in the void. The memoirist, like the poet and the novelist, must engage with the world, because engagement makes experience, experience makes wisdom, and finally it's the wisdom—or rather the movement toward it—that counts. "Good writing has two characteristics," a gifted teacher of writing once said. "It's alive on the page and the reader is persuaded that the writer is on a voyage of discovery." The poet, the novelist, the memoirist—all must convince the reader they have some wisdom, and are writing as honestly as possible to arrive at what they know. To the bargain, the writer of personal narrative must also persuade the reader that the narrator is reliable. In fiction a narrator may be—and often famously is—unreliable (as in *The Good Soldier*, *The Great Gatsby*, Philip Roth's Zuckerman novels). In nonfiction, never. In nonfiction the reader must believe that the narrator is speaking truth. Invariably, of nonfiction it is asked, "Is this narrator trustworthy? Can I believe what he or she is telling me?"

How do nonfiction narrators make themselves trustworthy? A question perhaps best answered by example.

"In Moulmein, in Lower Burma," George Orwell writes in "Shooting an Elephant," "I was hated by large numbers of people—the only time in my life that I have been important enough for this to happen to me. I was sub-divisional police officer of the town, and in an aim-less, petty kind of way anti-European feeling was very bit-ter. No one had the guts to raise a riot, but if a European woman went through the bazaars alone somebody would probably spit betel juice over her dress. As a police officer I was an obvious target and was baited whenever it seemed safe to do so. When a nimble Burman tripped me up on the football field and the referee (another Burman) looked the other way, the crowd yelled with hideous laughter. This happened more than once. In the end the sneering yellow faces of young men that met me every-where, the insults hooted after me when I was at a safe distance, got badly on my nerves. The young Buddhist priests were the worst of all. There were several thousands of them in the town and none of them seemed to have anything to do except stand on street corners and jeer at Europeans.

"All this was perplexing and upsetting. For at that time I had already made up my mind that imperialism was an evil thing and the sooner I chucked up my job and got out of it the better. Theoretically—and secretly, of course—I was all for the Burmese and all against their op-pressors, the British. As for the job I was doing, I hated it more bitterly than I can perhaps make clear. In a job like that you see the dirty work of Empire at close quarters. The wretched prisoners huddling in the stinking cages of the lock-ups, the grey, cowed faces of the long-term con-victs, the scarred buttocks of the men who had been flogged with bamboos—all these oppressed me with an intolerable sense of guilt. But I could get nothing into perspective. I was young and ill-educated and I had had to think out my problems in the utter silence that is imposed on every Englishman in the East. I did not even know that the British Empire is dying, still less did I know that it is a great deal better than the younger empires that are going to supplant it. All I knew was that I was stuck between my hatred of the empire I served and my rage against the evil-spirited little beasts who tried to make my job impossible. With one part of my mind I thought of the British Raj as an unbreakable tyranny, as something clamped down, in *saecula saeculorum*, upon the will of prostrate peoples; with another part I thought that the greatest joy in the world would be to drive a bayonet into a Buddhist priest's guts. Feelings like these are the normal by-products of imperialism; ask any Anglo-Indian official, if you can catch him off duty."

The man who speaks those sentences *is* the story being told: a civilized man made murderous by the situation he finds himself in. We believe this about him because the writing makes us believe it. Paragraph upon paragraph—composed in almost equal part of narration, commentary, and analysis—attests to a reflective nature now regarding its own angry passions with a visceral but contained distaste. The narrator records his rage, yet the writing is not enraged; the narrator hates Empire, yet his hate is not out of control; the narrator shrinks from the natives, yet his repulsion is tinged with compassion. At all times he is possessed of a sense of history, proportion, and paradox. In short, a highly respectable intelligence confesses to having been *reduced* in a situation that would uncivilize anyone, including you the reader.

This man became the Orwell persona in countless books and essays: the involuntary truth speaker, the one who implicates himself not because he wants to but because he has no choice. He is the narrator created to demonstrate the dehumanizing effect of Empire on all within its reach, the one whose presence alone—"I am the man, I was there"—is an indictment.

It was politics that Orwell was after: the politics of his time. That was the situation into which he interjected this persona: the one who alone could tell the story he wanted told. Orwell himself—in unaesthetic actuality—was a man often at the mercy of his own mean insecurities. In life he could act and sound ugly: revisionist biographies now have him not only a sexist and an obsessed anti-communist but possibly an informer as well. Yet the persona he created in his nonfiction—an essence of democratic decency—was something genuine that he pulled from himself, and then shaped to his writer's purpose. *This* George Orwell is a wholly successful fusion of experience, perspective, and personality that is fully present on the page. Because he *is* so present, we feel that we know who is speaking. The ability to make us believe that we know who is speaking is the trustworthy narrator achieved.

From journalism to the essay to the memoir: the trip being taken by a nonfiction persona deepens, and turns ever more inward.

One of the most interesting memoirists of our time is another Englishman, J. R. Ackerley. When Ackerley died in 1967, at the age of seventy-one, he left behind a remarkable piece of confessional writing he had been working on for the better part of thirty years. It is, ostensibly, a tale of family life. He was the son of Roger Ackerley, a fruit merchant known most of his life as "the banana king." This father was a large, easygoing, generous man, at once expansive and kindly but indirect in his manner, most indirect. Ackerley himself grew up to become literary and homosexual, absorbed by his own interests and secrets, given to hiding his real life from the family. After his father's death in 1929 Ackerley learned that Roger had lived a double life. All the time the Ackerleys were growing up in middle-class comfort in Richmond, the father was keeping a second family on the other side of London: a mistress and three daughters. The disclosure of this "secret orchard," as the Victorian euphemism had it, astounded Joe Ackerley to such a degree that he became obsessed with probing deeper into the obscurity of his father's beginnings. In time he became convinced that in his youth Roger had also been a male whore and that it was through the love of a wealthy man that he had gained his original stake in life.

This is the story J. R. Ackerley set out to tell. Why did it take him thirty years to tell it? Why not three? Because what I've told you was not his story; it was his situation. It was the story that took thirty years to get itself told.

Ackerley was, he thought, only putting together a

puzzle of family life. All I have to do, he said to himself, is get the sequence right and the details correct and everything will fall into place. But nothing fell into place. After a while he thought, I'm not describing a presence, I'm describing an absence. This is the tale of an unlived relationship. Who was he? Who was I? Why did we keep missing each other? After another while he realized, I always thought my father didn't want to know me. Now I see I didn't want to know him. And then he realized, It's not him I haven't wanted to know, it's myself.

My Father and Myself is little more than two hundred pages in length. Its prose is simple and lucid, wonderfully inviting from the first, now famous sentence, "I was born in 1896 and my parents were married in 1919." The voice that speaks that sentence will address with grace and candor whatever it is necessary to examine. From it will flow strong feeling and vivid intelligence, original phrasing and a remarkable directness. It's the directness that dazzles, coming as it does—and this is a minor miracle—from the exactly right distance: not too close, not too far. At this distance everyone and everything is made understandable, and therefore interesting. Because everyone and everything is interesting, we believe that the narrator is telling us all he knows.

Ackerley, as I have experienced him in writings *about* him, often seems nasty or pathetic; the Ackerley speaking here in *My Father and Myself* is a wholly engaging man, not because he sets out to be fashionably honest but because the reader feels him actively working to strip down the anxiety till he can get to something hard and true beneath the smooth surface of sentimental self-regard. It took Ackerley thirty years to clarify the voice that could tell his story—thirty years to gain detachment, make an honest man of himself, become a trustworthy narrator. The years are etched in the writing. Incident by incident, paragraph by paragraph, sentence by sentence, we have the glory of an achieved persona. Ackerley may not have the powers of a poet, but in *My Father and Myself* he certainly has the intent.

My trip to Egypt and the book that emerged from it now seem to me an embodiment of my own struggle to clarify, to release from anxiety the narrator who could serve the situation and find the story—a thing I was not then able to do. It was a time when my own psychological wishes were so mixed as to make it impossible for that instinct to be obeyed. I wanted at once both to clarify and to mystify. The compromised intent proved fatal. The problem was not detachment; the problem was I never knew who was telling the story. As a result, I never *had* a story. A dozen years after Egypt I set out to write a memoir about my mother, myself, and a woman who lived next door to us when I was a child. Here, for the first time, I struggled to isolate the story from the situation; here I taught myself what a persona is; and here I began to figure out what they all had to do with one another.

This story—the one about my mother, myself, and the woman next door—was based on an early insight I'd had that these two women between them had made me a woman. Each had been widowed young, each had fallen into despair; one devoted the rest of her life to the worship of lost love, the other became the Whore of Babylon. No matter. In each case the lesson being taught was that a man was the most important thing in a woman's life. I hated the lesson from early on, had resolved to get out and leave both it and the women behind. I did get out, but as time went on I discovered that I couldn't leave any of it behind. Especially not the women. Most especially not my mother. I had determined to separate myself from her theatrical self-absorption, but now, as the years accumulated, I saw that my hot-tempered and cutting ways were, indeed, only another version of her needy dramatics. I saw further that for both of us the self-dramatization was a substitute for action: a piece of Chekhovian unresolve raging in me as well as her. It flashed on me that I could not leave my mother because I had become my mother.

This was the story I wanted to tell without sentiment or cynicism; the one I thought justified speaking hard truths. The flash of insight I'd had—that I could not leave my mother because I'd become my mother—was my wisdom: a tale of psychological embroilment I wanted badly to trace out.

To tell that tale, I soon discovered, I had to find the right tone of voice; the one I habitually lived with wouldn't do at all: it whined, it grated, it accused; above all, it accused. Then there was the matter of syntax: my own ordinary, everyday sentence—fragmented, interjecting, overriding—also wouldn't do; it had to be altered, modified, brought under control. And then I could see, this as soon as I began writing, that I needed to pull back—*way* back—from these people and these events to find the place where the story could draw a deep breath and take its own measure. In short, a useful point of view, one that would permit greater freedom of association—for that of course is what I have been describing—had to be brought along. What I *didn't* see, and that for a long while, was that this point of view could only emerge from a narrator who was me and at the same time not me.

I began to correct for myself. The process was slow, painful, and, to my surprise, riddled with crippling self-doubt. I found a diary I had kept one summer ten years earlier; it contained information that I knew I could use. I opened the diary eagerly but soon turned away from it, stricken. The writing was soaked in a kind of girlish self-pity—"alone again!"—that I found odious. More than odious, threatening. As I read on, I felt myself being sucked back into its atmosphere, unable to hold on to the speaking voice I was working hard to develop. I threw the diary down in a panic, then felt confused and defeated. A few days later I tried again, but again felt myself going under. At last, I put it away.

One day—when I had been looking over an accumulation of pages possessed of what seemed to me the sufficiently right tone, syntax, and perspective—I opened the diary again, read in it a bit, laughed, got interested, even absorbed, and within minutes was making notes. With relief I thought, I'm not losing myself. Suddenly I realized there was no myself to lose. I had a narrator on the page strong enough to do battle for me. The narrator was the me who could not leave her mother because she had become her mother. She was not intimidated by "alone again." Nor, come to think of it, was she much influenced by the me who was a walker in the city, or a divorced middle-aged feminist, or a financially insecure writer. She was, apparently, only her solid, limited self—and she was in control. I saw what I had done: I had created a persona.

Devotion to this narrator—this persona—became, while I was writing the book, an absorption that in time went unequaled. I longed each day to meet up again with her, this other one telling the story that I alone—in my everyday person—would not have been able to tell. I could hardly believe my luck in having found her (that's what it felt like, luck). It was not only that I admired her style, her generosity, her detachment—such a respite from the me that was me!—she had become the instrument of my illumination.

Later, reading and re-reading Edmund Gosse, Geoffrey Wolff, Joan Didion, I went into a trance of recognition from which I don't think I ever emerged. I could see that their writing was "about" something in very much the same way that mine was. In each case the writer was possessed of an insight that organized the writing, and in each case a persona had been created to serve the insight. I became enraptured, tracing out the development of the persona in memoir after essay after memoir (it was out of this rapture that I realized I was a nonfiction writer). I began to read the greats in essay writing—and it wasn't their confessing voices I was responding to, it was their truth-speaking personae. By which I mean that organic whole-ness of being in a narrator that the reader experiences as reliable; the one we can trust will take us on a journey, make the piece arrive, bring us out into a clearing where the sense of things is larger than it was before.

Living as I now did with the idea of the nonfiction persona, I began to think better than I had before about the commonplace need, alive in all of us, to make large sense of things in the very moment, even as experience is overtaking us. Everywhere I turned in those days, I found an excuse for the observation that we pull from ourselves the narrator who will shape better than we alone can the inchoate flow of event into which we are continually being plunged. I remember once my then husband and I, and a friend of ours, went on a rafting trip down the Rio Grande. The river was hot and wild; sad, brilliant, remote; closed in by canyon walls, desert banks, snakes, and flash floods; on one side Texas, the other Mexico: a week after we'd been there, snipers on the Mexico side killed two people also floating on a raft. Later, we each wrote about the trip. My husband focused brightly on the "river rats" who were our guides, our friend soberly on the misery of illegal immigration, I morbidly on what strangers my hus-band and I had become. Reading these pieces side by side was in itself an experience. We had all used the river, the heat, the remoteness to frame our stories. Beyond that, how alone each of us had been, sitting there side by side on that raft, carving out of our separating anxieties the narrator who, in the midst of all that beauty and oppressiveness, would keep us company—and tell us what we were living through.

I began to see that in the course of daily life when, by my own lights, I act badly—confrontational, challenging, dismissive—I am out there on that raft before I have found the narrator who can bring under control the rushing onslaught of my own internal flux. When I am doing better, I am able to see that the flux is a situation. I stop churning around inside my own defensiveness; adopt a tone, a syntax, a perspective not wholly mine that allows me to focus on . . . what? the husband? the guides? the illegals? No matter. Any one of them will do. I become interested then in my own existence only as a means of penetrating the situation in hand. I have created a persona who can find the story riding the tide that I, in my unmediated state, am otherwise going to drown in.

■   ■   ■

It had been my intention when I began this book to provide an overview of nonfiction writing, but I very quickly saw that this was a task beyond my powers. The presence in a memoir or an essay of the truth speaker—the narrator that a writer pulls out of his or her own agitated and boring self to organize a piece of experience—it was about this alone that I felt I had something to say; and it was to those works in which such a narrator comes through strong and clear that I was invariably drawn.

The more I have read of memoir and essay, the more easily I have seen how long a history it has, this nonfiction persona, and how great is its capacity for adaptation to cultural change. As the last century wore on, the idea of "becoming oneself" altered—in literature as in life—almost beyond recognition. But whether that self is posited as whole or fragmented, real or alien, intimate or strange, the nonfiction persona—like the persona in novels and poems—has kept re-inventing itself with a strength and resourcefulness that are really quite remarkable. Whatever the story has been, as we approached the millennium, there's been a situation to contain it and a truth speaker to interpret it.

one THE ESSAY

If William Hazlitt hadn't awakened each morning crawling inside his own skin, he could not have written "On the Pleasure of Hating." If Virginia Woolf didn't have difficulty attaching herself to life, she would not have written "The Death of the Moth." If James Baldwin wasn't in perpetual violent struggle to bring the black and the white inside himself under control, there would be no "Notes of a Native Son." These pieces are the work of writers engaged at the deepest level with the essay. The form itself has released them into purposeful innerliness. Here the writing does not wander about on the page accumulating description for its own sake, or developing images independent of thought, or musing lyrically. The point of view originates in the nervous system and concentrates itself in the person of a narrator who causes the essay to move steadily forward, driven by an internal impetus that the reader can spot on page one: the obligation is to use the narrating self only to shape those associations that will provide drive and lead on to inner resolution. These writers might not "know" themselves—that is, have no more self-knowledge than the rest of us—but in each case—and this is crucial—they know who they are *at the moment of writing*. They know they are there to clarify in relation to the subject in hand—and on this obligation they deliver.

When writers remain ignorant of who they are at the moment of writing—that is, when they are pulled around in the essay by motives they can neither identify accurately nor struggle to resolve—the work, more often than not, will prove either false or severely limited. D. H. Lawrence's essay "Do Women Change?" is a case in point. Ostensibly a meditation on the cyclical recurrence throughout history of the modern, the piece in actuality is a denunciation of 1920s feminists. It fails, in my view, not because of its opinions but because Lawrence himself does not know what he is about. It is the writer's unknowingness that sinks the piece.

"They say the modern woman is a new type," he begins, on a note of sarcasm that never abates. "But is she? I expect, in fact I am sure, there have been lots of women like ours in the past . . . Women are women. They only have phases. In Rome, in Syracuse, in Athens, in Thebes, more than two or three thousand years ago, there was the bob-haired, painted, perfumed Miss and Mrs. of today . . . Modernity or modernism isn't something we've just invented. It's something that comes at the end of civilizations. Just as leaves in autumn are yellow, so the women at the end of every known civilization—Roman, Greek, Egyptian, etc.—have been modern . . .

"I saw a joke in a German paper—a modern young man and a modern young woman leaning on an hotel balcony at night, overlooking the sea. *He*: 'See the stars sinking down over the dark restless ocean!' *She*: 'Cut it out! My room number is 32!'

"That is supposed to be very modern: the very modern woman. But I believe women in Capri under Tiberias said '*Cut it out*' to their Roman and Campanian lovers in just the same way. And women in Alexandria in Cleopatra's time . . . They were smart, they were chic, they said . . . 'Oh, cut it out, boy! . . . My room number's thirty-two! Come to the point!'

"But the point, when you come to it, is a very bare little place, a very meager little affair. It's extraordinary how meager the point is once you've come to it . . . A lead pencil has a point, an argument may have a point, remarks may be pointed . . . But where is the point to life?

"Now, women used to understand this better than men . . . used to know that life is . . . not a question of points, but a question of flow. It's the *flow* that matters . . . And only the flow."

The language is strong, the feeling vivid, and the perspective coherent, but from start to finish the piece strikes a single unvarying note of blame and accusation that never advances, never diminishes. The ills and dissatisfactions of contemporary life are steadily traced to the mean, shallow willfulness of "emancipated" women, whose behavior is seen as an emanation from something profoundly "other." There is not a single moment in the piece—not a paragraph or a sentence—when the narrator sympathizes with his subject; that is, when he sees the modern woman as she might see herself, finds in himself that which would allow him to understand why she is as she is. It is this sympathy that creates a dynamic in writing, the one necessary to stimulate internal movement. In his novels Lawrence extends it to some of his most hated characters—most famously, the brutish father in *Sons and Lovers*—but in this essay we are presented steadily with the contemplation of a world in decay because of the women who remain relentlessly "other."

It is interesting to compare Lawrence with Hazlitt, a writer who also could have written "Do Women Change?" But if Hazlitt had written it, he would have been implicating himself continuously throughout his own rant. Repeatedly, we'd be given the line, the sentence, the image that would reveal Hazlitt's own anxieties about women. He would let us see the fear behind the anger, and this would make all the difference. We'd realize the writer is struggling to make sense of feelings whose complexity he acknowledges. The struggle alone would have made the subject vital.

In Hazlitt the head may be filled with blood, but the writing won't be. Neurotic as Hazlitt is, when he is writing his essays he owns his anger, and therefore he owns the material. Lawrence, on the other hand, is here possessed by his rage: it fills his head *and* his writing with blood; a thing that does not happen in his novels, where the engagement with women is equally visceral and equally antagonistic, yet is so imaginatively entered into that he cannot help but make the situation, and everyone in it, humanly understandable. In *Women in Love* and *Lady Chatterley's Lover* there are repeated rants about modern women—the ones who want to be men, the strong-willed ones, the ones who deny the primacy of the blood—but these rants do not dominate the work; they are in fact necessary for Lawrence to travel deeper into his subject: the struggle of men and women together. In the end, his characters share the situation, and we feel its power all the more because everyone is enmeshed. Fiction is the genre that lets Lawrence expand within himself: the proof that he is a born novelist but only on occasion an essayist. Here, in "Do Women Change?" he cannot manage it. Women remain an undynamic "them." It's the absence of dynamism that keeps the essay static, stifles its growth from within.

There is another writer who demonstrates repeatedly—and in exactly the same way as Lawrence—that he is an inspired writer of novels but not of nonfiction. V. S. Naipaul's vision of life is fundamentally cold, devoid in some important way of human warmth. Nevertheless, in his novels the coldness is made to burn. The viewpoint remains bleak, but the work opens out like some poisonous bloom; a mysterious empathy is in operation; the situation compels and the characters tell a story. In the nonfiction, however, the absence of sympathy is startling—and fatal. A perfect example of this striking differential is to be found in reading Naipaul's novel *Guerrillas* together with his essay "The Killings in Trinidad." Both are derived from the same newspaper story about a madman who became a self-styled black radical leader and ended up performing ritual murder on a number of his followers, including an upper-class Englishwoman who'd fallen under his spell. The novel is mysteriously injected with a power of dread that is so penetrating it endows the work with visionary properties: the situation becomes metaphoric. In the essay the principals—all of them, victims and victimizer alike—are presented like bugs under glass: shrunken, pinned, diminished. Naipaul's skin crawls with an untransformed disgust for his own subject. Disgust makes him shrink back. The shrinking attenuates the performance. In the end, the reader registers only the nastiness of the writer's feelings. He is standing too far back to achieve the right distance: the one necessary for engagement.

In all imaginative writing sympathy for the subject is

necessary not because it is the politically correct or morally decent posture to adopt but because an absence of sympathy shuts down the mind: engagement fails, the flow of association dries up, and the work narrows. What I mean by sympathy is simply that level of empathic understanding that endows the subject with dimension. The empathy that allows us, the readers, to see the "other" as the other might see him or herself is the empathy that provides movement in the writing. When someone writes a *Mommie Dearest* memoir—where the narrator is presented as an innocent and the subject as a monster—the work fails because the situation remains static. For the drama to deepen, we must see the loneliness of the monster and the cunning of the innocent. Above all, it is the narrator who must complicate in order that the subject be given life.

In fiction, a cast of characters is put to work that will cover all the bases: some will speak the author's inclination, some the opposition—that is, some represent an idea of self, some the agonistic other; allow them all their say, and the writer moves into a dynamic. In nonfiction, the writer has only the singular self to work with. So it is the other in oneself that the writer must seek and find to create movement, achieve a dynamic. Inevitably, the piece builds only when the narrator is involved not in confession but in this kind of self-investigation, the kind that means to provide motion, purpose, and dramatic tension. Here, it is self-implication that is required. To see one's own part in the situation—that is, one's own frightened or cowardly or self-deceived part—is to create the dynamic.

■ ■ ■

Three essays that demonstrate wonderfully the way self-implication can visibly shape a piece of non-fiction writing are Joan Didion's "In Bed," Harry Crews's "Why I Live Where I Live," and Edward Hoagland's "The Courage of Turtles." In each case, the piece begins in a tone of voice—one elegant, one swaggering, one reasonable—that announces a position. As the essay progresses this tone modulates—it softens, it inquires, it invites speculation. Modulation causes the narrator's position to alter. That process of alteration is at once the conduit for the story being told and, in some important way, the story itself. We are in the presence, in each instance, of a mind puzzling its way out of its own shadows—moving from unearned certainty to thoughtful reconsideration to clarified self-knowledge. The act of clarifying on the page is an intimate part of the metaphor.

For Joan Didion, ordinary, everyday anxiety is an organizing principle. Out of it she has created a depressed, quivering persona that serves her talent wonderfully, and has achieved at least one enduring novel (*Play It As It Lays*), as well as some of the finest essays in American literature. In her novels the anxiety is always in danger of becoming the story rather than serving the story, but in the essays, where a subject beyond the self must be intersected with—migraine headache, the Black Panthers, California and the American Dream—Didion's gorgeous nerves are brought under brilliant control. It is here, in this form, that her existential nervousness is developed with such artistry that insight transforms, and literature is made through the naked use of the writer's emotional disability. "In Bed," a famous piece on migraine headache, seems to me one of her small masterpieces.

Here's how the essay opens:

"Three, four, sometimes five times a month, I spend the day in bed with a migraine headache, insensible to the world around me. Almost every day of every month, between these attacks, I feel the sudden irrational irritation and the flush of blood into the cerebral arteries which tell me that migraine is on its way, and I take certain drugs to avert its arrival. If I did not take the drugs, I would be able to function perhaps one day in four. The physiological error called migraine is, in brief, central to the given of my life. When I was 15, 16, even 25, I used to think that I could rid myself of this error by simply denying it, character over chemistry. 'Do you have headaches *sometimes*? *frequently*? *never*?' the application forms would demand. 'Check one.' Wary of the trap, wanting whatever it was that the successful circumnavigation of that particular form could bring (a job, a scholarship, the respect of mankind and the grace of God), I would check one. '*Sometimes*,' I would lie. That in fact I spent one or two days a week almost unconscious with pain seemed a shameful secret, evidence not merely of some chemical inferiority but of all my bad attitudes, unpleasant tempers, wrongthink . . . For I had no brain tumor, no eyestrain, no high blood pressure, nothing wrong with me at all: I simply had migraine headaches, and migraine headaches were, as everyone who did not have them knew, imaginary."

The paragraph is clearly designed to forestall the suspicion that the narrator is a psychological malingerer, as those who suffer with migraine headache are commonly thought to be. Didion's elaborate syntax and elegant vocabulary demonstrate an intelligence that encourages the idea of self-command. The sentences are not only educated and the tone confident. How could anyone who uses phrases like the "physiological error called migraine" or "the sudden irrational irritation and the flush of blood into the cerebral arteries" be guilty of bringing on a hysterical headache?

This mentally well-heeled narrator goes on to tell us that migraine sufferers are genetically disposed, then gives us a medically sophisticated explanation of how it works and a detailed paragraph of description of what it feels like inside a migraine aura, again with an elegance of syntax and vocabulary that is its own claim to authority:

"The chemistry of migraine . . . seems to have some connection with the nerve hormone named serotonin, which is naturally present in the brain. The amount of serotonin in the blood falls sharply at the onset of migraine, and one [drug alone] seems to have some effect on serotonin . . .

"Once an attack is under way, however, no drug touches it . . . When I am in a migraine aura . . . I will drive through red lights, lose the house keys, spill whatever I am holding, lose the ability to focus my eyes or frame coherent sentences . . . The actual headache, when it comes, brings with it chills, sweating, nausea, a debility that seems to stretch the very limits of endurance. That no one dies of migraine seems, to someone deep into an attack, an ambiguous blessing."

In other words: Forces are at work well beyond the narrator's control.

Suddenly, in the middle of a paragraph about two-thirds of the way through the piece, we have a pair of sentences that indicate—ever so slightly—a shift in perspective: "All of us who have migraine suffer not only from the attacks themselves but from this common conviction that we are perversely refusing to cure ourselves by taking a couple of aspirin, that we are making ourselves sick, that we 'bring it on ourselves.' And in the most immediate sense, the sense of why we have a headache this Tuesday and not last Thursday, of course we often do." What's *this*? The merest hint of complication.

Swiftly the hint accumulates into a strong suspicion: "And I have learned now to live with it, learned when to expect it, how to outwit it, even how to regard it, when it does come, as more friend than lodger." More *friend* than lodger? Now where are we going?

The arrival of migraine, it seems, is *not* as random a

matter as we've been led to believe. There is, it appears, a pattern. One connected not to events of great disturbance but rather to the ordinary frustrations of everyday life. The ones that set off existential alarm and drive some people to drink, some to overeat, and some . . . well, to migraine: "Tell me that my house is burned down, my husband has left me, that there is gunfighting in the streets and panic in the banks, and I will not respond by getting a headache. It comes instead when I am fighting not an open but a guerrilla war with my own life, during weeks of small household confusions, lost laundry, unhappy help, canceled appointments, on days when the telephone rings too much and I get no work done and the wind is coming up. On days like that my friend comes uninvited."

Now the narrator's relation to migraine deepens rapidly. We see that for her, paradoxically, migraine is a painkiller. True, the painkiller itself is a horror. But when the need for relief is upon her, she is willing to induce one kind of anguish to rid herself of another: that of ordinary daily life.

The situation grows even richer. Not only is the narrator willing to make a holocaust in her brain, she now tells us, she actually quite *likes* the holocaust. In fact, it suits her right down to the ground: "Once it comes . . . I no longer fight it. I lie down and let it happen. At first every small apprehension is magnified, every anxiety a pounding terror. Then the pain comes, and I concentrate only on that. Right there is the usefulness of migraine, there in that imposed yoga, the concentration on the pain."

The headache is a purge. When the purge has spent itself, the world seems made anew, the narrator feels reborn: "For when the pain recedes, ten or twelve hours later, everything goes with it, all the hidden resentments, all the vain anxieties. The migraine has acted as a circuit breaker, and the fuses have emerged intact. There is a pleasant convalescent euphoria. I open the windows and feel the air, eat gratefully, sleep well. I notice the particular nature of a flower in a glass on the stair landing. I count my blessings."

These final sentences are as simple as the opening ones are complex. They mimic both the exhausted peace that follows the migraine itself and the narrator's act of slowing down internally to take in the undefended meaning of what it is she has really come to say.

Didion's "essay" into herself tells us a thing we all know to be true: that the power of everyday anxiety is ruthless: it makes us act against our own well-being, sometimes it even makes us court perversity, a thing we are ashamed of, can hardly bear to look at. Didion knows this bit of truth down to the bone. Shame is her quivering persona's middle name—shame leading on to confession and the need for punishment ("Right there is the usefulness of migraine . . ."). In this piece, she applies skillfully to a situation that seems born to contain it her signature piece of understanding by taking the reader on a journey of attitudes—from lofty remove to guarded self-deception to reluctant admission—that disentangles a knot of emotion as familiar as the back of any age-spotted hand.

■ ■

Harry Crews, a violently self-mythicizing Southerner, writes novels and stories set in the Georgia swamp culture from which he emerged. Here, in this essay, "Why I Live Where I Live," using his own unsurrogated self to speak again of his miserably divided feelings about "home," Crews also investigates a monumental sore spot in the shared psyche. Again, the essay opens with a vivid declaration of self:

"I can leave the place where I live a couple of hours before daylight and be on a deserted little strip of sand called Crescent Beach in time to throw a piece of meat on a fire and then, in a few minutes, lie back sucking on a vodka bottle and chewing on a hunk of bloody beef while the sun lifts out of the Atlantic Ocean (somewhat unnerving but also mystically beautiful to a man who never saw a body of water bigger than a pond until he was grown) and while the sun rises lie on a blanket, brain singing from vodka and a bellyful of beef, while the beautiful bikinied children from the University of Florida drift down the beach, their smooth bodies sweating baby oil and the purest kind of innocent lust (which of course is the rankest sort) into the bright air. If all that starts to pall—and what *doesn't* start to pall?—I can leave the beach and be out at the end of a dock, sitting in the Captain's Table eating hearts-of-palm salad and hot boiled shrimp and sipping on a tall, icy glass of beer while the sun I saw lift out of the Atlantic that morning sinks into the warm, waveless Gulf of Mexico. It makes for a hell of a day. But that isn't really why I live in the north-central Florida town of Gainesville."

The paragraph is a marvelous piece of aggressive swagger. The aggression lies in its rhythm (powerful and prolonged), an in-your-face description of appetite that announces, "This is who I am, take it or leave it," and ends on a note of rhetorical tease. Immediately the reader feels the note of challenge in the writer's posture—and is puzzled. Why is it there? What can it mean? Only one thing.

Insecurity dominates half the piece in the form of provocative observations, embarrassed ironies, self-conscious asides. For the next few paragraphs the sound of Crews's voice remains that of the challenging tease. He tells us that he uses the university library not as a scholar but as a seeker of odd bits of information (such as the car capacity of drive-in theaters in Bakersfield, California, in 1950); that it's a twenty-minute walk to his favorite bars (which saves him from "that abomination before the Lord, the car") and less than that to the house of a young woman who has been hypnotizing him for six years. But none of this—at the dismissive end of each paragraph—is why he lives in Gainesville.

We are in the presence of a man whose uncertainty is

announced repeatedly in phrases that alternate between the brash ("Some people get analyzed, I get hypnotized") and the hesitant ("Or, said another way: anyone other than I may find that the explanation does not satisfy"). Either way, the tone reveals the defensive posture of a man who clearly must rev himself up—in order to get down to it.

Then, unexpectedly and in the direct middle of the piece, halfway through a paragraph, he does. Telling us that he lives right in town on three acres of land thick with pines, oak, wild plum trees, and all manner of tangled, unidentifiable brush and that the only cleared space is the very narrow road leading down to the house because there are many things he absolutely refuses to do in this world, but the three things leading the list are wash his car, shine his shoes, and mow a lawn, he then tells us that the back wall of the room he works in at the rear of the house is glass, and "When I raise my eyes from the typewriter I look past an enormous bull bay tree through a thin stand of reeds into a tiny creek the banks of which are thick with the greenest fern God ever made. In my imagination I can follow that little creek upstream to the place where, after a long, circuitous passage, it joins the Suwannee River, and then follow the dark waters of the Suwannee upriver to the place where it rises in the nearly impenetrable fastness of the Okefenokee Swamp. Okefenokee: Creek Indian word for Land of the Trembling Earth, because most of the islands in the swamp— some of them holding hundreds of huge trees growing so thick that their roots are matted and woven as closely as a blanket—actually float on the water, and when a black bear crashes across one of them, the whole thing trembles."

Now the sentences open out—grave, direct, unbroken—from this long, lyrical passage I've always thought a metaphor for birth, leading directly into undefended memory. The narrator enters his own thought fully. No more ironies, no more asides. The need for self-protection has abated. He no longer fears the reader, because he has forgotten the reader. Now he will say what he has come to say: "Living here in North Florida, I am a little more than a hundred miles from where I was born and raised to manhood. I am just far enough away from the only place that was ever mine to still see it, close enough to the only people to whom I was ever kin in ways deeper than blood."

From this moment on the tone shifts permanently—and so does the balance between the writer's embarrassment and the undefended expanse of his reflection. What happens now is the really interesting development. The gravity and the insecurity change places. One takes over from the other. The insecurity is not vanquished, only subordinated. Embarrassment returns, and so does defensiveness, but these asides are now immensely reduced. The writer is so intent on his insight that he stands unprotected before the simple and profound thing it has taken all his life to understand: "I've tried to work—that is, to write—in Georgia, but I could not. Even under the best of circumstances, at my mama's farm, for instance, it was all too much for me. I was too deep in it, too close to it to use it, to make anything out of it. My memory doesn't even seem to work when I'm writing in Georgia. I can't seem to hold a story in my head. I write a page, and five pages later what I wrote earlier has begun to slide out of focus. If this is all symptomatic of some more profound malaise, I don't want to know about it and I certainly don't want to understand it.

"Living here in Gainesville seems to give me a kind of geographic and emotional distance I need to write. I can't write if I get too far away. I tried to work on a novel in Tennessee once and after a ruined two months gave it up in despair. I once spent four months near Lake Placid in a beautiful house lent to me by a friend—perfect place to write—and I didn't do a damn thing but eat my guts and look out the window at the mountains."

In other words: If you don't leave home you suffocate, if you go too far you lose oxygen.

The essay becomes an exercise in the meaning and value of watching a writer conquer his own sense of threat to deliver himself of his wisdom. Only slowly—as in life itself—has Crews been able to come to it. By making the essay mirror the difficulty he has in facing the thing he is embarrassed by, and frightened of admitting to, Crews gradually leads us to a deeper insight: the *unwillingness* with which we—all of us—arrive at self-understanding. It is here, in the imitation of that reluctance, that we locate the metaphoric value of the piece. Again, the way the narrator writes *himself* is the thing being written about. One echoes the other.

■   ■

The most absorbing instance among the three of how nonfiction makes use of the "other" in oneself is to be found in Edward Hoagland's "The Courage of Turtles," a self-investigating piece disguised as a nature essay. As a rule, I don't read nature writing, because I hardly ever get it. The metaphor always feels strained and the sensibility foreign—that hushed, saintly "quiet" in the narrating voice. "The Courage of Turtles," however, is the work of the most urban naturalist in America. By the end of this piece Hoagland's "quiet" comes to seem distinctly *dis*quieting.

The narrator of this essay, a man in his forties or fifties, grew up in the country and watched his beloved woods turn into a suburban development. He remembers how the world around him grew as he grew—from a two-acre pond across the road to a larger one a mile away to a lake-sized one up in the mountains—and then imploded:

"For a long while the developers stayed away, until the drought of the mid-1960s . . . convinced the local water company that [Mud Pond] really wasn't a necessity as a catch basin . . .; so they bulldozed a hole in the earthen dam, bulldozed the banks to fill in the bottom, and landscaped the flow of water that remained to wind like an English brook and provide a domestic view for the houses which were planned. Most of the painted turtles of Mud Pond, who had been inaccessible as they sunned on their rocks, wound up in boxes in boys' closets within a matter of days. Their footsteps in the dry leaves gave them away as they wandered forlornly. The snappers and the little musk turtles, neither of whom leave the water except once a year to lay their eggs, dug into the drying mud for another siege of hot weather, which they were accustomed to doing whenever the pond got low. But this time it was low for good; the mud baked over them and slowly entombed them."

So begins an essay whose calm neutrality of voice is its most striking quality. Never once will the sound of this voice vary—not from its leisurely beginning to its startling last line—moving smoothly along, accumulating beneath a surface so uninflected as very nearly to persuade the reader that the narrator is detached to a point of indifference. But then we learn that when he moved to the city, he decided to make turtles stand in for all the animals he'd never again have in his life on a daily basis. Here's why turtles:

"Turtles cough, burp, whistle, grunt and hiss, and produce social judgments. They put their heads together amicably enough, but then one drives the other back with the suddenness of two dogs who have been conversing in tones too low for an onlooker to hear. They pee in fear when they're first caught, but exercise both pluck and optimism in trying to escape, walking for hundreds of yards within the confines of their pen, carrying the weight of that cumbersome box on legs which are cruelly positioned for walking. They don't feel that the contest is unfair; they keep plugging, rolling like sailorly souls—a bobbing, infirm gait, a brave, sea-legged momentum—stopping occasionally to study the lay of the land. For me, anyway, they manage to contain the rest of the animal world. They can stretch out their necks like a giraffe . . . loom . . . like [a] hippo . . . browse . . . like a cow . . . They have a penguin's alertness, combined with a build like a brontosaurus when they rise up on tiptoe. Then they hunch and ponderously lunge like a grizzly going forward."

The pleasures of baby turtles are particularly great—they often die young, but while they live are "like puppies . . . a puzzle in geometrics . . . self-directed building blocks, propping themselves on one another in different arrangements, before upending the tower"—as are those of Hoagland's own sculptured wood turtle, who gazes at the passing ground with a hawk's eyes and mouth, strikes like a mongoose, and climbs on his lap to eat bread or boiled eggs.

These descriptions—written against the sound of Hoagland's remarkably distant voice—are a joy to read. The intentness with which the narrator observes the turtles persuades us that, oh yes—what a relief!—after all, he *does* have feeling, he's just more comfortable speaking in a voice free of emotion (*you* know how it is with some men), but *certainly*, he's attached to the turtles, they are his connection.

So the piece ambles along, and somehow time—in the

city, in the narrator—passes. At last the disquisition on Hoagland and the turtles winds down; concludes itself, so to speak; and we come to the final sequence:

"I was walking on First Avenue when I noticed a basket of living turtles in front of a fish store . . . I looked and was touched to discover that they appeared to be wood turtles, my favorites, so I bought one. In my apartment I looked closer and realized that in fact this was a diamond-back terrapin, which was bad news . . . He drank thirstily but would not eat and had none of the hearty, accepting qualities of wood turtles. He was morose, paler in color, sleeker and more Oriental . . . Though I felt sorry for him, finally I found his unrelenting presence exasperating. I carried him, struggling in a paper bag, across town to the Morton Street Pier on the Hudson River . . . He was very surprised when I tossed him in; for the first time in our association, I think, he was afraid. He looked afraid as he bobbed about on top of the water, looking up at me from ten feet below . . . I recognized that I must have done the wrong thing . . . [T]he river was salty, but it was also bottomless; the waves were too rough for him, and the tide was coming in, bumping him against the pilings underneath the pier. Too late, I realized that he wouldn't be able to swim to a peaceful inlet in New Jersey, even if he could figure out which way to swim. But since, short of diving in after him, there was nothing I could do, I walked away."

That's it. There is no more. The piece has arrived.

The first time I read this essay I stared at the final line

and thought, This is really about Hoagland and women: "I picked her up on the street. She was just my type. Took her home. Oh. Made a mistake. Wrong one. Let her bob around somewhere else in the world. Oh. Made another mistake. She can't swim. Too bad. But, hey. What could *I* do?"

The second time I read it I thought, This is about the loss of feeling in all of us as the presence of nature becomes more attenuated.

The third time I read it I thought, It's about both.

Once that final line is absorbed, it echoes back throughout the piece. The reader realizes that the man who's using turtles as a stand-in for human intimacy has been there from the very beginning. He tells us clearly enough: He had grown up loving all the animals, expecting to live in peace with his fellow creatures. But the developers had just kept coming. And the creature within had become entombed in the mud. Yet he, like the turtle, had survived: cold, quiet, alert. Containing within himself not multitudes but a sufficiency of response just large enough to avoid the charge of unnatural.

It is Hoagland's complexity—the intentness of his observation coupled with the elegance of his withdrawal—that gives this essay its inner life. His mixed feelings provide the texture, and the drama. Patiently and "quietly," they lead us into the starkness of solipsism. The turtles have taught the narrator that nothing outside himself is quite real to him.

The metaphor is worthy of Thoreau, another coldly brilliant self-examiner traveling to and from the pond, also barely escaping the charge of unnatural.

■　　■　　■

Sometimes in an essay the simple *presentation* of a fractured self becomes a thesis by virtue of the writer's talented insistence that confession alone has an existential claim on our attention. Seymour Krim is an ardent practitioner of such writing.

Krim is a Jewish Joan Didion. His work personifies the joys and pitfalls of writing that turns openly on the organization of the writer's own anxiety. In a headnote on him that can't be improved upon, Phillip Lopate observed that in the 1950s Krim developed an essay-writing persona—"that of the quintessential New Yorker: street-smart, neurotic, ambitious, self-mocking, manic yet depressed or downbeat"—and through this persona he made an identity out of his breakdowns, his hungers, and his envy of those who had achieved worldly success—very much in the style of the great nineteenth-century English eccentrics in essay writing (Lamb, Hazlitt, etc.) who also developed ardent, ailing, self-involved voices speaking to us at vivid and voluble length. The ability of these voices to compose themselves into monologues that entertain and instruct rather than weary and exhaust is an extraordinary achievement.

At the time that Krim was writing—in the 1950s, the era of the Man in the Gray Flannel Suit *and* the Beat Generation—his was a voice imbued at once with the bohemian longing to break free of middle-class constraint and with the psychological distress that precludes resolution of will. At his best he could make the division within seem emblematic of some fatal split in America itself. Failure—both his own and that of the national dream—became a major theme of Krim's through the simple expedient of his endlessly crying out on the page his own depressed, daydreaming self. In too many pieces, the noble complaint runs away with him, and the writing is reduced to a disheveled rant: tiresome and pathetic. But when he brings it under control, Krim's work becomes a dazzling example of what American writing in particular can do with the personal essay. In "For My Brothers and Sisters in the Failure Business" he pulls it together with rare power.

Here is the essay in part:

"At 51, believe it or not, or believe it and pity me if you are young and swift, I still don't know truly 'what I want to be.' I've published several serious books. I rate an inch in *Who's Who in America*. I teach at a so-called respected university. But in that profuse upstairs delicatessen of mine I'm as open to every wild possibility as I was at 13, although even I know that the chances of acting them out diminish with each heartbeat . . .

"That's because I come from America, which has to be the classic, ultimate, then-they-broke-the-mold incubator of not knowing who you are until you find out. I have never really found out and I expect what remains of my life to be one long search party for the final me. I don't kid myself that I'm alone in this, hardly, and I don't really think that the great day will ever come when I hold a finished me in my fist and say here you are, congratulations. I'm talking primarily about the expression of that me in the world, the shape it takes, the profile it zings out, the 'work' it does.

"You may sometimes think everyone lives in the crotch of the pleasure principle these days except you, but you have company, friend. I live under the same pressures you do. It is still your work or role that finally gives you your definition in our society, and the thousands upon thousands of people who I believe are like me are those who have never found the professional skin to fit the riot in their souls. Many never will. I think what I have to say here will speak for some of their secret life and for that other sad America you don't hear too much about. This isn't presumption so much as a voice of scars and stars talking. I've lived it and will probably go on living it until they take away my hotdog.

". . . America was my carnival at an earlier age than most and I wanted to be everything in it that turned me on . . . Democracy means democracy of the fantasy life, too, there are no cops crouching in the corridors of the brain . . . Yet those of us who have never really nailed it down, who have charged through life from enthusiasm to enthusiasm, from new project to new project, even from personality-revolution to personality-revolution, have a secret also . . .

"Our secret is that we still have an epic longing to be more than what we are, to multiply ourselves, to integrate all the identities and action-fantasies we have experienced, above all to keep experimenting with our lives all the way to Forest Lawn . . . Let me say it plainly: Our true projects have finally been ourselves. It's as if we had taken literally the old cornball Land of Opportunity slogan and incorporated it into the pit of the being instead of the space around us; and fallen so much in love with the ongoing excitement of becoming, even the illusion of becoming, that our pants often fall down and reveal our dirty skivvies and skinny legs. The laughter hurts, believe me, but it doesn't stop us for very long. We were hooked early.

". . . What unites [me and all those like me] is that we never knew except in bits and pieces how to find a total expression, appreciated by our peers, in which we could deliver ourselves of all the huge and contradictory desires we felt within. The country was too rich and confusing for us to want to be one thing at the expense of another. We were the victims of our enormous appreciation of it all.

". . . [I]t was a beautiful, breathless eagerness for all the life we could hold inside, packed layer on layer like a bulging quart container of ice cream . . . That's what this democracy was for us, a huge supermarket of mass man where we could take a piece here and a piece there to make our personalities for ourselves instead of putting up with what was given at the beginning.

"But this lovely idea became for some of us a tragedy, or at least a terrible confusion that wasn't counted on at the beginning . . .

"I was living in Europe at the time . . . when the dirty American word 'failure' winged its way across the water and hit me where it hurts . . . Maybe I never had a choice, and would have been an uncertain performer at whatever I did, but my decision to aim at the stars had been a conscious one and this was the way it was being weighed on the common man's do-it-or-shut-up scale . . .

"But if you are a proud, searching 'failure' in this society, and we can take ironic comfort in the fact that there are hundreds of thousands of us, then it is smart and honorable to know what you attempted and why you are now vulnerable to the body blows of those who once saw you robed in the glow of your vision and now only see an unmade bed and a few unwashed cups on the bare wooden table of a gray day."

The pleasure of the piece (and the profit as well) lies in the rich, sure speed of its language; language that is riding the fast-forward movement of American idiom, its street-smart, slangy intelligence mimicking the whole preoccupation with youth: both Krim's and America's. Idiomatic language always feels young—in any language it makes the adrenaline shoot right up—but none more so than the American. The sheer *sound* of it is young. And no one knows how to work that sound better than Krim. Just listen to his beautiful use of it:

that profuse upstairs delicatessen of mine

in the crotch of the pleasure principle

the riot in their souls

a voice of scars and stars

until they take away my hotdog

there are no cops crouching in the corridors of
the brain

all the way to Forest Lawn

all the life we could hold . . . packed layer on
layer like a bulging quart container of ice cream

the dirty American word "failure" winged its
way across the water and hit me where it hurts

being weighed on the common man's do-it-or-
shut-up scale

[those who now see my life as] only . . . an
unmade bed and a few unwashed cups on the
bare wooden table of a gray day

A middle-aged writer of American prose is crying out
in a voice forever young, "I'm no longer young!"

Inscribed in the essay—in the rhythm and structure of
its idiomatic insight—is all the deep downward movement
of Krim's yearning, and the sweet sad stoppage of his ar-

rest. He is the man who sees it all, understands it all—has been over it, under it, around it, times without number—but still he fails to take in his own experience. Like America itself, he is besotted with "self-creation." For both the man and the culture, this translates into an adolescent longing that life remain filled with untested promise. As Americans, Krim insists, we are nostalgic for *promise* even while we are young: as though we are born with romantic regret for beginning again. Our literature is indeed saturated with it—from Walt Whitman to Raymond Carver. And here is Seymour Krim—as though lit from within—his essay-writing persona a rich embodiment of the condition itself. Through his speaking voice the extraordinary energy of "failure American-style" surrounds and enters us, moving swiftly and with exhilaration straight to the heart.

■　　■

While I was reading "For My Brothers and Sisters in the Failure Business," I happened on the work of Jean Améry, a European journalist who in the 1960s wrote a remarkable series of essays on aging. Améry was a Holocaust survivor who settled in Belgium after the war intending to write books. He went to work as a journalist—just for a while, he thought—and, somehow, twenty years passed with him doing work he despised. Then, in his fifties, he wrote a successful wartime memoir and gave up journalism to write as he had always wanted to write. Now, however, he found age weighing fearfully on his soul. Growing old, he concluded, was worse than Auschwitz. The terror of the concentration camp, he said, was "less filled with internal *horror* and *anguish* than the experience of aging." The horror and the anguish became his subject.

In these essays Améry sets out to describe with an absence of sentiment that borders on the nihilistic exactly what he is experiencing. The idea is to look with an unblinking eye on every major aspect of a condition that can be understood by no one not actually living through it. Améry, however, will be our Marco Polo, returned from a foreign land to which all must journey to report on what awaits us. The report is one of unredeeming loss.

To begin with, he tells us, there is the matter of time. When we are young we stand in the middle of both space *and* time, but as we grow older our sense of space disappears and time alone crowds in on us, becomes in fact a characteristic of daily existence; we think about time all the time.

Then we become strangers to ourselves. We look in the mirror and are startled, if not shocked, by the face that looks back at us. This is a shock from which we never recover; it, too, is with us day after day (the irony here being that it is only now that we actually see ourselves with any clarity).

The natural world becomes alien as well: who wants to look at a mountain that one can no longer climb? or swim in water that denies us the exactly right temperature?

Worse yet is what Améry calls cultural aging. We no longer feel at one with the world around us. New developments in art, politics, and fashion puzzle, anger, or discomfort us. We cannot see our own experience reflected back in them.

On and on Améry goes. Relentlessly he argues a repetitious and unsparing view of age as a punishment from the gods:

"A. [stares into the mirror each morning, unable to make her peace with the face that stares back at her]: what she witnesses in her morning ritual [the changed face in the mirror] has nothing or little to do with . . . her earlier self and even later better days . . . Perhaps the strongest component of weariness is just this alienation from herself, this discrepancy between the young self she has brought along with her through the years and the self of the aging woman in the mirror. But in the same breath and in the same tick of time it becomes obvious to her, if she just perseveres in front of the mirror and does not turn away from the glass . . . that she . . . is *closer* to herself, with all her weariness and intimate familiarity than ever before, and that in front of her mirror image, now a stranger to her, she is condemned to become more and more oppressively herself . . . [T]his discovery of the clasping together of alienation from oneself and an increased sense of self . . . is the fundamental experience of all those aging persons who simply have the patience to persevere in front of the mirror, who can summon up the courage not to let themselves be chased away . . . who do not internalize the conventional judgment of others and submit to it . . . It is the ambiguity of aging that A. is discovering and in which she is establishing herself . . .

"We are constantly in the clutches of the ambiguity of alienation from, and familiarity with, ourselves, of self-weariness and self-seeking. The former always drowns out the latter initially at the point where thought turns into speech: That's supposed to be who I am? they ask, those sick with aging and sick of it as well, whenever they look into the mirror or realize again and again while walking, running, or climbing that the world is becoming their adversary, that their body, which has carried them and their selves, is becoming a corpus that weighs upon them within and is itself a weight outside . . . in aging the body becomes more and more *mass* and less and less *energy*. This mass . . . stands in resistance to the old self, which has been preserved by time and has been constituting itself in time, as the hostile new ego, foreign and, in the exact meaning of the word, odious . . .

"[A]ging is not a 'normal condition' for the aging person . . . Actually, it is quite definitely a sickness, indeed a form of suffering from which there is no hope of recovery . . . Aging is an *incurable* sickness, and because it is a form of suffering it is subject to the same phenomenal laws as any other acute hardship that afflicts us at some particular stage of life . . .

"The ambiguity of alienation from oneself and familiarity with oneself in aging—by which we must not forget for one minute that aging is a form of suffering and that

61

we experience it as such—this ambiguity consists not only in the fact that we feel our body as a mortal shell while at the same time this shell is taking root in us more and more; it also becomes manifest in our social ego's contradiction of everything else that is formed from our suffering body, of the body-ego that is both our clothing and what we clothe . . .

"Alienation from oneself becomes alienation from being, no matter how faithfully we still attend to the day, fill out our tax declaration, go to the dentist. Were we saying that in aging the world becomes our denial . . .

"For a few years A. has been disturbed by the cooling off of what he once called his feeling for landscape . . . Specifically, he became conscious in nature more than in the city of how the world, which he still had possessed as a part of his person, had become the denial of this person . . . the others climbed the mountain, swam in the lakes, strolled about in the valleys: he was expelled and thrown back on himself . . . The hostility of the landscape . . . was only conscious to A. now as the contradiction of his person. He began to avoid nature. Now he has become thoroughly alienated from it and withdraws to where the challenge of a world that has come to be his denial no longer humiliates him every hour: to his room . . .

"We could just as easily have said that we are already about to be the negation of our self. Day and night cancel each other out in twilight . . .

"In the life of every human being there is a point in time . . . where each discovers that one is only what one is.

All at once we realize that the world no longer concedes us credit for our future, it no longer wants to entertain seeing us in terms of what we *could* be . . . We find ourselves . . . to be creatures without potential. No one asks us any longer, 'What do you want to do?' . . . The aging, whose accomplishments were already counted and weighed, have been condemned. They have lost even if they've won, that is, even if their social existence . . . is assessed at a high market value. Break-ups and upheavals no longer lie on their horizon."

A man of wide reading and philosophical bent, Améry brings to bear on these textured pieces the concreteness of journalism, the insight of literature, the analysis of history. The voice is dry, patient, reasonable, and very European. It is a voice—from Montaigne to Céline—that we have been hearing for half a millennium: a voice of egocentric "realism," the kind that shades easily into the *sur*real.

There is much to quarrel with in these essays. For some they read like warmed-over existentialism; for others the truth they deliver is very partial. I myself remain unpersuaded on many scores. I am older now than Améry was when he was writing, and I share none of his conclusions. Yet for me, these essays are an essence of persona. The negativism embodied in them is so intense, so insistent that I for one feel penetrated by the strength of its vision. Améry's focus, like acid on zinc, bites deep into the grain of his experience. He is a scientist at the microscope staring into a cell slide he can make no sense of with a killer epidemic raging at his back. He stands where I think

I will never stand. Yet I feel, powerfully, *him* standing there, *him* looking into the void. It is the depth of his concentration under duress that compels. More than compels, exhilarates. The exhilaration is startling; draws me up short; makes me understand better why I am being drawn.

While Améry was intoning his measured European "we's," I kept hearing Seymour Krim calling out his exclamation point "I's." Something vital united this unlikely pair. Despite the inner tumult native to the American and the dramatic history inflicted on the European, each man, as he entered middle age, seemed overcome by the realization that he had not done the work necessary to attain inner freedom (that, of course, is what is driving Améry's obsession with age), the work Lawrence was referring to when he said, "Man is free only when he is doing what the deepest self likes, and knowing what the deepest self likes, ah! that takes some diving." Central to both Krim and Améry was that each one considered himself a failure because neither—by his own lights—had engaged with his own deepest self. Here was a pair of men widely separated by culture, geography, and focus—yet both haunted by the inability to have faced down their own youthful anxieties, to have made themselves dive.

It struck me then how each of them had made this common sorrow transmute into essays of great particularity by making out of himself a persona absolutely at one with the deeper "idiom" of his own culture— Krim's youthful preoccupation with success so American, Améry's Proustian exercise in loss equally European. Each had paid strict attention to the actuality of his own experience, at the same time framing that experience in the formative mind-set of the culture in which he had come of age.

Shortly after reading Krim and Améry, I read a pair of essays on marriage—again, one by an American and one by a European—that struck a similar chord. Each of these essays has a narrator who speaks strictly for herself and, at the same time, out of an inner environment clearly at one with the culture into which the writer had been born. These elements combined, it seemed to me, to form a rich compound that provided the basis for yet one more evocative example of how inventive an exercise the art of self-implication could be.

What follows is simply the flavor of both essays.

FOR BETTER AND WORSE
by Lynn Darling

"I was married ten years ago, on a brazenly warm day in January, from my father's house, in a dress my mother made, with the same blithe blindness that sends a bungee jumper off a bridge.

"I was thirty-four—not a young bride but about right for my narrow slice of the world: baby boomer, middle-class professional, exquisitely self-referential. My kind didn't marry young. In our twenties, marriage was about as hip as Tupperware parties . . .

"I married the man I married because I liked his version of myself better than my own. I married him because I loved him, because I felt more real with him than I had felt with anyone else . . . I married him because he loved Ford Madox Ford, because he made the perfect martini, because we could fight and the walls did not fall down, because he was more at home with being a man than any man I knew, because he shouldered responsibility with deceptive ease, and because his eyes welled up with tears elicited by the everyday grace of ordinary people.

"They were no better and no worse, as reasons go, than any others I've heard for getting married: Such decisions hinge on a trick of the light, a tick of the clock, the urgent call of an errant and unreliable heart . . .

"The first Valentine's Day after we were married, my husband gave me bath towels. They were red towels, what are called 'seconds'—the kind with snagged threads and other flaws that consign them to the bargain shelves. There was a bow on the shopping bag by way of gift wrapping.

"I remember that I cried when I unfolded them. I was furious; the towels were a metaphor that blotted out the sun, shrieked across the reassuring hum of a gradually gathering dailiness. It was a romantic high noon, an emotional and historic accounting in which my husband was found sadly wanting. Now I would say that we were not really married then; we were still in teen-romance mode—he loves me, he loves me not—still riveted by the high drama and pitched emotion of courtship and passion, in which a passing glance can detonate a sudden emotional danger.

"What I can't remember any more is why I was so angry. The reasoning must have been something like this: I have staked everything on this man, and he is not what I thought; he is not the man who cries when he reads Ford Madox Ford. I have defined myself in terms of this choice, this man, and this is the kind of man he is, the Kind Who Gives Towels.

"I smile now when I remember this story, set back in the phase when marriage is still a mirror, reflecting back only one's carefully constructed, easily shattered conceit. Now my husband gives me bath towels every Valentine's Day, and every Valentine's Day I laugh. It has become part of our mythology. But the laughter is its own edgy commentary on how things have changed, how we have changed each other, how the two people who smile at this joke are indelibly stained with each other's expectations and disappointments, how who we are is a composite of who we might have been refracted through the lens of whom we married. The laughter is a counterpane, covering the lumps we've dealt each other, the scars left from the various surgeries we've performed on each other, the enthusiasms dampened so that a couple might emerge . . .

"When I was single, I equated marriage with drowning: Your identity disappeared, your privacy was invaded, your self submerged. After I married, I found out that I was right; what I hadn't known was how much of an amphibian I could be . . .

"All marriages are mended garments. In marriage, you don't make it all better; you get over it. By marrying, Robert Louis Stevenson warned, 'you have willfully introduced a witness into your life . . . and can no longer close the mind's eye upon uncomely passages, but must stand up straight and put a name upon your actions.' Because if you don't, she will . . .

". . . There is a depth of intimacy to domesticated love-making that nothing can equal; yet there are times when the idea of making love to just one person for the rest of your life can make your head hurt. So where does that leave us, apart from staring at the ceiling at three o'clock in the morning or at each other over the remnants of the tiramisu? I don't know. Marriage, when it works, is a mystery made up of such a complicated ebb and flow of affection, admiration, fury, ritual, and gradually unfolding understanding that with the right person it's not a bad way to live a life. But if it means giving up fire and first kisses, then it seems like more than a little death. So one is left with a simple choice: self-denial or betrayal, contentment or ecstasy, earth or fire, the lady or the tramp.

"Most of us choose not to take the risk while leaving open the loophole, in much the same way that I continue not to smoke only because I pretend that I haven't smoked my last cigarette . . .

"But then it is a Sunday afternoon. My husband and I are playing Monopoly Junior with our daughter. Chet Baker's trumpet fills the room. I hated jazz when I was single, but now our marriage is steeped in this music, in the ways I have changed and the things I've come to know, in exasperation and elegance, in the poetry of dailiness, in the solace of each other's company. I see the ways my husband saved me, the ways I saved him. There is still pain in the phantom limbs lost in the making of this marriage, but in that moment the loss seems a manageable part of the trade. I see only the courage and kindness that marriage elicits, not the cost, and it seems to me that it gives us our only chance to be heroes. I want the song Baker is playing never to end."

HE AND I
by Natalia Ginzburg

"He always feels hot, I always feel cold. In the summer when it really is hot he does nothing but complain about how hot he feels. He is irritated if he sees me put a jumper on in the evening.

"He speaks several languages well; I do not speak any well . . .

"He has an excellent sense of direction, I have none at all . . .

"He loves the theatre, painting, music, especially music. I do not understand music at all, painting doesn't mean much to me and I get bored at the theatre. I love and understand one thing in the world and that is poetry . . .

"He loves travelling, unfamiliar foreign cities, restaurants. I would like to stay at home all the time and never move.

"All the same I follow him on his many journeys. I follow him to museums, to churches, to the opera. I even follow him to concerts, where I fall asleep . . .

"He is not shy; I am shy. Occasionally however I have seen him be shy. With the police when they come over to the car armed with a notebook and pencil. Then he is shy, thinking he is in the wrong.

"And even when he doesn't think he is in the wrong. I think he has a respect for established authority. I am afraid of established authority, but he isn't. He respects it. There is a difference. When I see a policeman coming to fine me I immediately think he is going to haul me off to prison. He doesn't think about prison; but, out of respect, he becomes shy and polite . . .

"He likes tagliatelle, lamb, cherries, red wine. I like minestrone, bread soup, omelettes, green vegetables.

"He often says I don't understand anything about food, that I am like a great strong fat friar—one of those friars who devour soup made from greens in the darkness of their monasteries; but he, oh he is refined and has a sensitive palate . . .

"Everything I do is done laboriously, with great

difficulty and uncertainty. I am very lazy, and if I want to finish anything it is absolutely essential that I spend hours stretched out on the sofa. He is never idle, and is always doing something; when he goes to lie down in the afternoons he takes proofs to correct or a book full of notes; he wants us to go to the cinema, then to a reception, then to the theatre—all on the same day. In one day he succeeds in doing, and in making me do, a mass of different things, and in meeting extremely diverse kinds of people. If I am alone and try to act as he does I get nothing at all done, because I get stuck all afternoon somewhere I had meant to stay for half an hour, or because I get lost and cannot find the right street, or because the most boring person and the one I least wanted to meet drags me off to the place I least wanted to go to.

"If I tell him how my afternoon has turned out he says it is a completely wasted afternoon and is amused and makes fun of me and loses his temper; and he says that without him I am good for nothing.

"I don't know how to manage my time; he does . . .

"I don't know how to dance and he does.

"I don't know how to type and he does . . .

"I am very untidy. But as I have got older I have come to miss tidiness, and I sometimes furiously tidy up all the cupboards . . . My tidiness and untidiness are full of complicated feelings of regret and sadness. His untidiness is triumphant. He has decided that it is proper and legitimate for a studious person like himself to have an untidy desk.

"He does not help me get over my indecisiveness, or the way I hesitate before doing anything, or my sense of guilt . . . Sometimes he does the shopping to show me how quickly he can do it . . .

"And so—more than ever—I feel I do everything inadequately or mistakenly. But if I once find out that he has made a mistake I tell him so over and over again until he is exasperated. I can be very annoying at times.

"His rages are unpredictable, and bubble over like the head on beer. My rages are unpredictable too, but his quickly disappear whereas mine leave a noisy nagging trail behind them which must be very annoying—like the complaining yowl of a cat.

"Sometimes in the midst of his rage I start to cry, and instead of quietening him down and making him feel sorry for me this infuriates him all the more. He says my tears are just play-acting, and perhaps he is right. Because in the middle of my tears and his rage I am completely calm.

"I never cry when I am really unhappy . . .

"When he was a young man he was slim, handsome and finely built; he did not have a beard but long, soft moustaches instead, and he looked like the actor Robert Donat. He was like that about twenty years ago when I first knew him, and I remember that he used to wear an elegant kind of Scottish flannel shirt. I remember that one evening he walked me back to the *pensione* where I was living; we walked together along the *Via Nazionale*. I already felt that I was very old and had been through a great deal and had made many mistakes, and he seemed a boy to me, light years away from me. I don't remember what we talked about on that evening walking along the *Via Nazionale*; nothing important, I suppose, and the idea that we would become husband and wife was light years away from me. Then we lost sight of each other, and when we met again he no longer looked like Robert Donat, but more like Balzac. When we met again he still wore his Scottish shirts but on him now they looked like garments for a polar expedition; now he had his beard and on his head he wore his ridiculous crumpled woollen hat; everything about him put you in mind of an imminent departure for the North Pole. Because, although he always feels hot, he has the habit of dressing as if he were surrounded by snow, ice and polar bears; or he dresses like a Brazilian coffee-planter, but he always dresses differently from everyone else.

"If I remind him of that walk along the *Via Nazionale* he says he remembers it, but I know he is lying and that he remembers nothing; and I sometimes ask myself if it was us, these two people, almost twenty years ago on the *Via Nazionale*, two people who conversed so politely, so urbanely, as the sun was setting; who chatted a little about everything perhaps and about nothing; two friends talking, two young intellectuals out for a walk; so young, so educated, so uninvolved, so ready to judge one another with kind impartiality; so ready to say goodbye to one another for ever, as the sun set, at the corner of the street."

What divides these essays is easily described. The American's is the work of a journalist interweaving social observation and personal testimony, claiming the experience of marriage for herself and her contemporaries, the voice one of urban sophistication riddled through with longing for the what might have been, its tone both ironic and lyrical; the Italian's that of a novelist producing a bill of particulars (her case rests on "he does this, I do that"), the voice all uninflected minimalism, its tone forthright and seemingly without judgment (deep into the is-ness of what is). But beneath the irony and the smart-ass nostalgia, Darling's essay mounts with singular gravity; and beneath the pose of bare-bones matter-of-factness, Ginzburg moves steadily toward an ending that leaves the reader staring into space. We see in her final paragraphs a pair of strangers, etched in memory, having little or nothing to do with the people that "he and I" have become: strangers who fell randomly together when they could just as easily have fallen randomly apart but didn't; and so the randomness got cemented into history and became marriage.

In each case the writer is discovering the mysterious in

the familiar. Looking hard at an experience on which everyone in the world has an opinion, she sees that she is a principal in a beloved situation about which she has serious misgivings. As a principal, she also sees that she is complicitous. It's the complicitousness that, again in each case, holds the writer's attention, makes her keep digging. The more she digs, the more surprised she becomes. Fixed even. Stunned, in fact. Stunned by what it actually *means*: being married. In both essays, the stun is central to the action of the piece. How extraordinary, when one comes to think of it, this compelling need to bend ourselves out of shape, rationalize a trade-off, endure an intermingling of gratitude and antagonism that will *never* separate out—all in order that we might mate. Our own eyes begin to widen as the starkness of the double bind sinks in.

It's the randomness, we now realize, that in both essays is the line of influence running strongly beneath the surface of the prose—the shock of it, the struggle over a lifetime to justify, account for, make sense of: why *him*? why not the one who came before, or the one after? And beneath the randomness—at the heart of the appraising "I" in each essay—a faint but distinct irritation in the voice permeating the very air that each piece breathes. This irritation flavors every nuance, every inflection, every slight tonal change. In it the reader hears the barely conscious, primal expectation—still alive in the amazement beneath the sophistication—that two *should* have been as one. It is an essence of persona in these pieces, that irritation; and the anxiety it speaks to, of whether or not to go it alone.

It was reading the essays together that had done it. If I hadn't read Darling first, then Ginzburg, then Darling again, I don't think I would have seen the depth and complexity of feeling that drives both pieces forward. As with Krim and Améry, the persona of each writer clarified, for me, each in relation to the other.

I realized that I was experiencing a familiar pleasure in an unfamiliar setting: the pleasure of reading in literary context: what one feels routinely when reading poems or novels but is hardly ever aware of, I think, with essays. Open a work of fiction or of poetry, and immediately a landscape of literature comes up on the inner screen of a reader's mind. Writers large and small take their place on that landscape, many of them connected with a signature piece of experience: Colette and erotic love, Stendhal and worldly longing, Willa Cather and the unlived life. Read a book dominated by passion or politics or quiet desperation, and—whether one is conscious of it or not—behind the reading moment—or rather inside it, under it, over it—floats, hovers, intrudes Colette, Stendhal, Cather. Their company is the context within which our present read is invariably made richer.

When I read Améry and heard Krim echoing in my ears, I now realized, I was beginning to see that *essays* could be read the way poems or novels are read, inside the same kind of context, the one that enlarges the relation between life and literature. Tolstoy, Flaubert, and

H. G. Wells notwithstanding, I will not again think of marriage without flashing on both Lynn Darling and Natalia Ginzburg.

■　　■　　■

"**He and I**" is an essay rather than a memoir because the writer is using her persona to explore a subject other than herself: in this case, marriage. If it had been a memoir, the focus would have been reversed. Ginzburg would have been using marriage precisely to explore—illuminate, define—herself. That would have been her intention. Her simple intention, I might add.

A perfect bridge between the essay and the memoir is James Baldwin's "Notes of a Native Son," a piece in which the writer takes a deep breath, inhaling the experience of himself in the world, then expels it through a viewpoint of such *complex* intentionality that the intersection between the self and the world becomes one of nearly perfect equality: neither being served at the expense of the other so that at one and the same time a subject is explored and self-definition is pursued. The opening paragraphs of Baldwin's famous essay demonstrate perfectly what I mean:

"On the 29th of July, in 1943, my father died. On the same day, a few hours later, his last child was born. Over a month before this, while all our energies were concentrated in waiting for these events, there had been, in Detroit, one of the bloodiest race riots of the century. A few hours after my father's funeral, while he lay in state in the undertaker's chapel, a race riot broke out in Harlem. On the morning of the 3rd of August, we drove my father to the graveyard through a wilderness of smashed plate glass . . .

"I had not known [him] very well. We had got on badly, partly because we shared, in our different fashions, the vice of stubborn pride . . . He had lived and died in an intolerable bitterness of spirit and it frightened me, as we drove him to the graveyard through those unquiet, ruined streets, to see how powerful and overflowing this bitterness could be and to realize that this bitterness now was mine."

What we have here is a narrator who is going to give us the history of the morning of August 3, 1943—Harlem in the middle of the Second World War—exactly as it entered into him, creating a composite portrait that will lend equal weight to his childhood landscape of black America and to the particular figures standing on it. He will lay this intricacy out so well that we will stand behind his eyes: see and feel it as he then saw and felt it; understand it as he now understands it. To achieve this doubleness of viewpoint—that of his very own self, that of his very shared blackness—he must plot a story, one that begins with the man in the coffin, the grim preacher father, who, we are told, was handsome:

"Handsome, proud, and ingrown, 'like a toe-nail,' somebody said . . . He could be chilling in the pulpit and indescribably cruel in his personal life and he was certainly the most bitter man I have ever met; yet it must be said that there was something else in him, buried in him, which lent him his tremendous power and, even, a rather crushing charm. It had something to do with his blackness, I think—he was very black—with his blackness and his beauty, and with the fact that he knew that he was black but did not know that he was beautiful . . . [All this] sometimes showed in his face when he tried, never to my knowledge with any success, to establish contact with any of us . . . I do not remember, in all those years, that one of his children was ever glad to see him come home."

The isolation inside the father is extended to the world: "He spent great energy and achieved, to our chagrin, no small amount of success in keeping us away from the people who surrounded us, people who had all-night rent parties to which we listened when we should have been sleeping, people who cursed and drank and flashed razor blades on Lenox Avenue . . . [As for whites, needless to say, they] would do anything to keep a Negro down . . . The best thing was to have as little to do with them as possible."

Baldwin had hated and resented the raging loneliness of the father, thought him deluded about the world (it *couldn't* be that bad), and had determined to experience himself in a place free of his deforming influence. The summer he was eighteen he'd left Harlem for the first time, gone to work in a war plant in New Jersey, and then, to his horror, had experienced the white world much as had his father before him:

79

"That year . . . lives in my mind as though it were the year during which . . . I first contracted some dread, chronic disease, the unfailing symptom of which is a kind of blind fever, a pounding in the skull and fire in the bowels. Once this disease is contracted, one can never be really carefree again, for the fever, without an instant's warning, can recur at any moment. It can wreck more important things than race relations. There is not a Negro alive who does not have this rage in his blood—one has the choice, merely, of living with it consciously or surrendering to it. As for me, this fever has recurred in me, and does, and will until the day I die.

". . . I saw nothing very clearly [that year] but I did see this: that my life, my *real* life, was in danger, and not from anything other people might do but from the hatred I carried in my own heart."

As the summer of 1943 draws on, the Baldwin family settles down to a period of awful waiting: the father's imminent death, the mother's last confinement. The narrator sees that the world around him is also settling down:

"All of Harlem, indeed, seemed to be infected by waiting. I had never before known it to be so violently still . . . I had never before been so aware of policemen . . . everywhere . . . Nor had I ever been so aware of small knots of people. They were on stoops and on corners and in doorways, and what was striking about them, I think, was that they did not seem to be talking . . . Another thing that was striking was the unexpected diversity of the people who made up these groups . . . large, respectable, churchly matrons standing on the stoops or the corners with their hair tied up, together with a girl in sleazy satin whose face bore the marks of gin and the razor, or heavy-set, abrupt, no-nonsense older men, in company with the most disreputable and fanatical 'race' men, or these same 'race' men with the sharpies, or these sharpies with the churchly women . . . [S]omething heavy in their stance seemed to indicate that they had all, incredibly, seen a common vision, and on each face there seemed to be the same strange, bitter shadow."

What they had all seen was the suffering they'd been hearing about in letters coming back to Harlem from friends and relatives in the army who'd been sent to training camps in the South. And what everyone on the street was now feeling was a great powerlessness, coupled with "that panic which can scarcely be suppressed when one knows that a human being one loves is beyond one's reach, and in danger." So bad was this feeling (about the black soldiers in Southern camps) that most people, that summer on Lenox Avenue, experienced "a peculiar kind of relief when they knew that their boys were being shipped out of the south, to do battle overseas . . . [as though] the most dangerous part of a dangerous journey had been passed and . . . now, even if death should come, it would come with honor and without the complicity of their countrymen. Such a death would be, in short, a fact with which one could hope to live."

The very next paragraph begins:

"It was on the 28th of July, which I believe was a

Wednesday, that I visited my father for the first time during his illness and for the last time in his life. The moment I saw him I knew why I had put off this visit so long. I had told my mother that I did not want to see him because I hated him. But this was not true. It was only that I *had* hated him and I wanted to hold on to this hatred."

The essay's singular insight is established: they hate us, we hate ourselves. The letters coming back from the training camps in the South, the riot in Detroit, the gatherings on the corners, the narrator's father dying alone in that "intolerable bitterness of spirit." We understand in our nerve endings: it is all one; they define one another.

So where does this leave the narrator? Hating whites and wishing them all dead? Of course not. "In order really to hate white people," he now observes, "one has to blot so much out of the mind—and the heart—that this hatred itself becomes an exhausting and self-destructive pose. But this does not mean, on the other hand, that love comes easily: the white world is too powerful, too complacent, too ready with gratuitous humiliation, and, above all, too ignorant and too innocent for that. One is absolutely forced to make perpetual qualifications and one's own reactions are always canceling each other out. It is this, really, which has driven so many people mad, both white and black."

At this point we feel keenly the derangement inherent in racism, and see clearly that our narrator has no intention of losing his mind. On the contrary, he has been writing to clear it: to make it function; to make it *count*. Interwoven throughout this impassioned piece of testament laced through with a novelist's sense of event is the long argument with himself that Baldwin at his best was to conduct in print for years to come:

"It began to seem that one would have to hold in the mind forever two ideas which seemed to be in opposition. The first idea was acceptance, the acceptance, totally without rancor, of life as it is, and men as they are . . . [T]he second idea was of equal power: that one must never, in one's own life, accept these injustices as commonplace but must fight them with all one's strength. This fight begins, however, in the heart and it now had been laid to my charge to keep my own heart free of hatred and despair. This intimation made my heart heavy and, now that my father was irrecoverable, I wished that he had been beside me so that I could have searched his face for the answers which only the future would give me now."

It was an ingenious dynamic that Baldwin was devising in "Notes of a Native Son," a back-and-forth between "us" and "them," between the white and the black in himself, that got worked into the large building blocks of his thought, and then into his very sentence structure. Inside the elastic tension of that sentence Baldwin found he could be everything he had to be—rational, humane, and cutthroat—all at the same time. Not for our sake, for his own.

At the end of "Notes of a Native Son" when Baldwin

says he's stuck with having to keep two opposing ideas in his head at the same time, we realize that what he's talking about is the burden of civilization: of *being* civilized. We also realize that this is the real preoccupation of the essay, one that is reflected in the writing: in its remarkable steadiness of voice, its tight control over rhetoric, its freedom from emotionalism. As he writes, the narrator is becoming the very thing he is writing about: he is civilizing himself. It is his tone of voice that carries the message: more than carries it: becomes it. The narrator's tone of voice *is*, in fact, the true subject of the piece.

Orwell's "Shooting an Elephant" and Baldwin's "Notes of a Native Son" have a powerful commonality. Both turn on race, both continuously interweave the personal with the political, and both are dominated by a murderous truth-speaking voice: the narrator using himself to demonstrate that none are exempt from the dehumanizing effects of racism. At the same time, in neither case is the writing pulled around by the emotions that actually drive the essay. Orwell, too—composing paragraph after paragraph of measured narrative, analysis, and commentary so that the writing itself is continually bringing the heat of reaction under control—is holding it all together through the hard, clear, civilizing voice he was making distinctively his own; "civilizing" being the operative word.

The story here, as in other personal essays, is the large sense that the writer is making of his own participation in the situation. But in these pieces the balance between the world and the self has more than equalized, and sent the narrator shifting downward and inward. In both "Notes of a Native Son" and "Shooting an Elephant" a rare depth of inquiry into the self suffuses the prose. It's the depth of inquiry that guides the personal narrative from essay into memoir.

two THE MEMOIR

Thirty years ago people who thought they had a story to tell sat down to write a novel. Today they sit down to write a memoir. Urgency seems to attach itself these days to the idea of a tale taken directly from life rather than one fashioned by the imagination out of life.

For many, the development is puzzling. Everywhere—among those who read and those who write—people are asking, Why memoir? And why now? What has happened over the past decades to account for the vivid shift in interest, from one genre to another, that is overtaking the common impulse, alive at all times, to shape one's own experience through writing? What does the shift mean? How long will it last? How far can it go? The questions are rhetorical, the answers strictly speculative. Here's my own take on why memoir now.

To begin with, modernism has run its course and left us stripped of the pleasures of narrative: a state of reading affairs that has grown oppressive. For many years now our novels have been all voice: a voice speaking to us from inside its own emotional space, anchored neither in plot nor in circumstance. To be sure, this voice has spoken the history of our time—of lives ungrounded, trapped in interiority—well enough to impose meaning and create literature. It has also driven the storytelling impulse underground. That impulse—to tell a tale rich in context, alive to situation, shot through with event and perspective—is as strong in human beings as the need to eat food and breathe air: it may be suppressed but it can never be destroyed.

As the twentieth century wore on, and the sound of voice alone grew less compelling—its insights repetitive, its wisdom wearisome—the longing for narration rose up again, asserting the oldest claim on the reading heart, the measure of whose deprivation is to be taken in the literalism of the newly returned "tale." What, after all, could be more literal than The Story of My Life now being told by Everywoman and Everyman?

At the same time that the power of voice alone has been dwindling, an age of mass culture paradoxically much influenced by modernism has emerged on a scale unparalleled in history, and today millions of people consider themselves possessed of the right to assert a serious life. A serious life, by definition, is a life one reflects on, a life one tries to make sense of and bear witness to. The age is characterized by a need to testify. Everywhere in the world women and men are rising up to tell their stories out of the now commonly held belief that one's own life signifies. And everywhere, civil rights movements and the therapeutic culture at large have been hugely influential in feeding the belief. In this country alone forty years of liberationist politics have produced an outpouring of testament from women, blacks, and gays that is truly astonishing. Following quickly in the wake of political interpretation has come the echoing response of lives framed by pedestrian chaos: alcohol, domestic violence, sexual disorder, the premature death of children. These, too, it appears, signify. These, too, have a story to tell, a catastrophe to relate, a memoir to write.

But memoir is neither testament nor fable nor analytic transcription. A memoir is a work of sustained narrative prose controlled by an idea of the self under obligation to lift from the raw material of life a tale that will shape experience, transform event, deliver wisdom. Truth in a memoir is achieved not through a recital of actual events; it is achieved when the reader comes to believe that the writer is working hard to engage with the experience at hand. What happened to the writer is not what matters; what matters is the large sense that the writer is able to *make* of what happened. For that the power of a writing imagination is required. As V. S. Pritchett once said of the genre, "It's all in the art. You get no credit for living."

That idea of the self—the one that controls the memoir—is almost always served through a single piece of awareness that clarifies only slowly in the writer, gaining strength and definition as the narrative progresses. In a bad memoir, the line of clarification remains muddy, uncertain, indistinct. In a good one, it becomes the organizing principle—the thing that lends shape and texture to the writing, drives the narrative forward, provides direction and unity of purpose. The question clearly being asked in an exemplary memoir is "Who am I?" Who exactly is this "I" upon whom turns the significance of this story-taken-directly-from-life? On that question the writer of memoir must deliver. Not with an answer but with depth of inquiry.

When Rousseau observes, "I have nothing but myself to write about, and this self that I have, I hardly know of what it consists," he is saying to the reader, "I will go in search of it in your presence. I will set down on the page a tale of experience just as I think it occurred, and together we'll see what it exemplifies, both of us discovering as I write this self I am in search of." And that was the beginning of memoir as we know it.

The "I" that Rousseau had in mind has undergone vast changes in definition, but for more than a century it strongly resembled what Willa Cather could in the 1930s still call "the inviolable self"; by which she meant some core being at the center in whose company we breathe free; with whom we feel neither isolated nor exiled nor bent out of shape; something we call our real selves. This is an "I" that cannot be explained or illuminated in terms of generic disaster (blizzards, blindness, incest, addiction) or the randomness of political misery (class, race, sex). It is the "I" the existentialists had in mind when they spoke of "becoming," the one that in our time is called authentic.

Modern memoir posits that the shaped presentation of one's own life is of value to the disinterested reader only if it dramatizes and reflects sufficiently on the experience of "becoming": undertakes to trace the internal movement away from the murk of being told who you are by the accident of circumstance toward the clarity that identifies accurately the impulses of the self that Cather calls inviolable. An early-twentieth-century memoir that performs brilliantly on this score is Edmund Gosse's *Father and Son*.

Gosse was born in London in 1849 to Philip and Emily Gosse, members of the Plymouth Brethren, a fundamentalist Christian sect of fanatical severity; at birth he was dedicated by his parents to "the Service of the Lord." He grew up, however, to become a literary critic of prodigious output and influence, and an avid social climber who enjoyed urban life to the full. In his fifties he was made a Fellow of the Royal Society of Literature, receiving honors abroad as well as at home; two years before he died, he was knighted. But the work for which Gosse had been so rewarded during his lifetime was destined to perish with him; after his death, it no longer spoke to a world now unresponsive to its dominating Victorianism.

In 1907, when he was fifty-eight years old, Gosse published *Father and Son*, the memoir that has secured him his posterity. From the outset the book was seen as remarkable. Unexpectedly, he had produced a hybrid work framed in Victorian sentences but governed by the truth-speaking voice of the new century. In its own way, it did what *Sons and Lovers* would do when it was published six years later in 1913. Lawrence's great novel exploded upon contemporary consciousness with an openly modernist presentation of what it means—what it *really* means—to spend one's childhood struggling to realize what he called "the deepest self" (that is, the self freed of conventional restraint) at the same time that one is coming to understand that the restraint is erotically enmeshed with a vital parent (in his case, famously, the mother). While Gosse was not Lawrence, either in temperament or in mission, he nonetheless also complicated wonderfully his own early history with a portrait of parental relations that was unmistakably romantic in character.

The story Gosse tells begins with a father (a marine biologist of some reputation) and a mother (a talented writer of religious tracts) whose mutual devotion is the reading of Scripture. Together, they pray, read, and talk Scripture from one end of the day to the other: not because they must but because it pleases them. The companionateness of Philip and Emily is unusually strong. True, the house is silent and the atmosphere austere, but within that context the parents are warm with each other and with their child. Riddled through as it is with worldly self-denial, life in the Gosse household is not at all unhappy.

When Edmund is seven years old, his mother is stricken with cancer and dies. The father mourns her loss bitterly, weeping openly and praying hypnotically. His pain breaks the little boy's heart. The gloom and the isolation in the house deepen, but so also does the connection between the impressionable child and the largehearted man. A somber pathos envelops them. In their grief and confusion these two cling to each other.

A year later Philip Gosse and his son move to a remote village on the coast of Devon, where Philip becomes the leader of the local Brethren. One year after that, at the age of ten, under the gentle but relentless pressure of his father's messianic will, Edmund undergoes public baptism and becomes a boy preacher in the church. To have done otherwise would have been to cause his father a distress the young Edmund cannot bear to contemplate.

Yet beneath the acquiescence a resistance has been steadily building, one he can hardly name. He knows only that praying wearies him; that he loves the poetry of the liturgy but not its injunctions; that he is drawn to biblical stories but not to their moral conclusions; that in church he is bored and his mind wanders. He does not feel God. He wants to, but he does not. What he does feel—and this stronger and stronger each year—is a growing love of language and of narrative: the language of the imagination, the tale of human emotion hidden in the prose. In short, he is discovering in himself the man of letters he is to become, and this without friends, without conversation, without worldly experience. Alone, within the silent embrace of his own unspoken thought, through the remarkable companionship he finds in his own growing consciousness, Gosse encounters a "self" at the center whose demands slowly overtake him.

These are the two major elements that organize the prose: Edmund's discovery of his own consciousness, and the powerful bonding between himself and his fanatical father. The two are put in place early, the first being established with one of the most compelling descriptions in English literature of the discovery of the inner life. One morning in his sixth year, he tells us, he and his mother were alone in the morning room when his father came in and announced some fact about something that had happened in the street:

"I was standing on the rug, gazing at him, and when he made this statement, I remember turning quickly, in embarrassment, and looking into the fire. The shock to me was as that of a thunderbolt, for what my Father had said 'was not true.' My Mother and I, who had been present at the trifling incident, were aware that it had not happened exactly as it had been reported to him. My Mother gently told him so, and he accepted the correction. Nothing could possibly have been more trifling to my parents, but to me it meant an epoch." A week or two later Edmund accidentally ruins a piece of his father's garden and sees that his own culpability is going to go undetected: "My Father, as a deity, as a natural force of immense prestige, fell in my eyes to a human level. In future, his statements about things in general need not be accepted implicitly."

The child is thrown into turmoil. If Papa does not know everything, he asks himself, then what *does* he know? And what is one to do with what he says? How is one to decide what to believe and what not to believe? In the midst of this confusion he suddenly realizes that he's talking to himself:

"[O]f all the thoughts which rushed upon my savage and undeveloped little brain at this crisis, the most curious was that I had found a companion and a confidant in myself. There was a secret in this world and it belonged to me and to a somebody who lived in the same body with me. There were two of us, and we could talk with one another. It is difficult to define impressions so rudimentary, but it is certain that it was in this dual form that the sense of my individuality now suddenly descended upon me, and it is equally certain that it was a great solace to me to find a sympathizer in my own breast."

Within the year the remarkably self-communing child will become the sole friend of the devastated father. And here is the second element being put in place:

"As I now look back upon that tragic time, it is for him that my heart bleeds . . . My Mother, in her last hours, had [promised that she was passing] through a door, into a world of light, where we should presently join her . . . He held this confidence and vision steadily before him, but nothing availed against the melancholy of his natural state. He was conscious of his dull and solitary condition, and he saw, too, that it enveloped me. I think his heart was, at this time, drawn out towards me in an immense tenderness. Sometimes, when the early twilight descended upon us in the study, and he could no longer peer with advantage into the depths of his microscope, he would beckon me to him silently, and fold me closely in his arms. I used to turn my face up to his, patiently and wonderingly, while the large, unwilling tears gathered in the corners of his eyelids. My training had given me a preternatural faculty of stillness, and we would stay so, without a word or a movement, until the darkness filled the room. And then, with my little hand in his, we would walk sedately downstairs, to the parlour, where we would find that the lamp was lighted, and that our melancholy vigil was ended. I do not think that at any part of our lives my Father and I were drawn so close to one another as we were in that summer of 1857. Yet we seldom spoke of what lay so warm and fragrant between us."

The reader becomes aware of a number of things at once. The father's will is oppressive, but the father himself is not oppressive; the atmosphere is stifling, but the boy is not stifled; the emotional air is close and the space confining, but always—from the beginning—there is room *enough* for the boy to walk around inside himself, to take himself in, to puzzle things out. This air, this space is created by the steady, liquid flow of the father's tender affection.

The tenderness is an amazement. Here we have a man without imagination or real intellect (in the Darwinian crisis Philip Gosse foolishly wrote a book arguing that God put the fossils in the rocks), a man given over to a suffocatingly excluding doctrine, determined that the son's life will duplicate his own; and yet he holds the boy to him with the unfailing gift of an empathic heart. This father never shuts this child out: not when the wife dies, not when he suffers public intellectual humiliation, not when he worries about money, salvation, or the incapacities of the Brethren. At all times he folds the child to his breast. Gosse re-creates this inner circumstance full strength so that we will understand how large are the stakes here, grasp the immensity of his having ultimately to say to this man, "I am not you. Whatever it is that I am, it is not you."

The immensity is the story; the rest is situation. That this son must come into his own by making war not on a parent who is willful and self-involved (which he is) but on one filled with the tender regard that alone gives a growing creature the ability to declare itself (which he also is). *This* is the thing the reader is meant to register; this is the narrator's wisdom. It is the betrayal of love that is required in order that one become.

The sympathy with which Gosse enters into the spirit of his father's life is the great achievement of the book: it is the thing that allows him ultimately to enter himself. From the beginning, the memoir is soaked through with eloquent descriptions of that against which he will at last define himself: the keenness and fervor of the father at prayer, the passionate preoccupation with Sacred Prophecy, the ecstatic sermonizing, the all-in-allness of the religious quest, its unmistakable depth of character.

Concomitantly runs a record of the slowly separating self charted through the illicit discovery of literature. Made to read the Epistle of the Hebrews, the child is stirred by the mysterious beauty of the language; set to studying Latin, he registers the astonishing pleasure of Virgil's voice; given an adventure tale meant only to increase his knowledge of geography, he is nearly toppled by the narrative excitement of *Tom Cringle's Log*; when he finds his way to Shakespeare and the Romantic poets, there is no going back. Literature makes steady inroads on the growing boy, who comes early to honor its association with "my innate and persistent self. Meek as I seemed, and gently respondent, I was always conscious of that innermost quality which I had learned to recognize in my earlier days . . . that existence of two in the depths who could speak to one another in inviolable secrecy."

At the end of this memoir we do not know everything there is to know about Edmund Gosse, not by a long shot—of Gosse the Victorian aesthete or the literary man-about-town, nothing. We know only one thing: we know what it was to be his father's son. That is, we know the man who is recording the struggle and the value of the separating self: the man who is speaking.

■   ■   ■

Written only twenty years later in the century, Agnes Smedley's *Daughter of Earth* strikes an altogether different note on the register of "becoming," one in which the writer describes a condition of life cruelly hostile to the very idea of an inner self, whole or otherwise, and does so through a narrator whose speaking voice will become painfully resonant of the brutishness she is documenting. Above all, it is a voice that identifies wholly with the culture from which it springs:

"What I [write] is not a work of beauty, created that someone may spend an hour pleasantly; not a symphony to lift up the spirit, to release it from the dreariness of reality. It is the story of a life, written in desperation . . . I write of the joys and sorrows of the lowly . . . For thirty years I have lived, and for these years I have drunk from the wells of bitterness . . . [T]here are times when . . . [t]o die would have been beautiful. But I belong to those who do not die for the sake of beauty. I belong to those who die from other causes—exhausted by poverty, victims of wealth and power, fighters in a great cause. A few of us die, desperate from the pain or disillusionment of love, but for most of us 'the earthquake but discloseth new fountains.' For we are of the earth and our struggle is the struggle of earth . . ."

So begins a masterful piece of primitive writing: crude, hot, immediate; its images cropped, the picture it forms all foreground, without perspective and without margin. The protagonist in *Daughter of Earth* moves across a stripped-down landscape where inner life is an outpost in the wilderness and she a creature who must make herself out of chalk and clay and human rubble.

Agnes Smedley was born in 1892 in Missouri into a family of poverty and ignorance. Her people were farmers who labored in the field from morning till night; endured drought, tornadoes, and failed crops. The father was a man "with the soul and imagination of a vagabond": handsome, restless, a teller of tall tales. The mother was beautiful for a minute; after that, a hard-worked farmwife old at thirty. Within a few years of marriage the parents are quarreling bitterly. He wants to break away, make money, feel alive: "There were but three or four festivals a year. The rest of the time he had to follow the lone plow . . . stumbling over the clods with his bare feet. He wanted to wear shoes all the year." The mother spits back at him that he sticks to nothing, is always complaining, always telling stories that aren't true and singing songs instead of working.

The quarrels deepen. He curses, she weeps, he storms out, she's left staring at the kitchen table: "But he won at last, for we all went away. And from that moment on our roots were torn from the soil and we began a life of wandering, searching for success and happiness and riches that always lay just beyond—where we were not. Only since then have I heard the saying: 'Where I am not, there is happiness.'"

The family becomes part of the drifting, grifting nineteenth-century underclass perpetually moving west in that astonishing national "wander" that got the country built through the unremitting labor of loggers, miners, teamsters, with all their brute strength and inner chaos and all that stupid cunning in them that was never any match for those who held the money power. Like thousands of others, Smedley's father is a hopeless loser, an ignorant, frightened blusterer helpless before a world he cannot understand much less prevail against. In time the songs and the stories die out in him; he becomes a bully, a drunk, and a wife beater: "Her tears . . . they embittered my life!"

Throughout the girl's childhood the Smedleys keep moving . . . Kansas, Missouri, Colorado . . . from one mining camp to another . . . always working like dogs, always being cheated, always surviving. "Existence meant only working, sleeping, eating what or when you could, and breeding. For amusement there was the saloon for the men; for the women, nothing. A book was a curiosity, a newspaper a rarity; to read was a recreation of the rich."

When a strike occurs among the miners, the ignorance is more desperate than the anger: "Resentful everybody was, but we bowed our heads and waited for the strikes to pass, and in the end we obeyed those who paid us wages and thereby gave us the right to live. We said 'Yes, sir!' and 'Thank you, sir' for we knew that this was necessary . . . Too many years have flown since those days, too many storms have swept over my own life, for me to recall fully the depths of non-knowing that was ours. Often in later years I heard men and women say that 'people get what they deserve,' and always my mind has swept back to our canyon-like existence. 'Deserve' is the word which the possessors use as a weapon against those they dispossess. The darkness of not-knowing—who can realize what that means unless he has lived through it! Those who speak of 'deserving people' are the most ignorant of all. Because the world of knowledge was far removed from us, we in our canyon reacted instead of thinking."

Capitalism is the unmistakable enemy of this *Grapes of Wrath* population, but terrible as the life is for everyone, men and women alike, very young the girl sees that for a woman it is really slavery. To be independent and respectable *and* a woman is clearly an impossibility: the future holds either marriage or prostitution. By the time Agnes is twelve, prostitution is looking better to her than marriage:

"After school hours, on Saturdays and on holidays, I helped neighboring women wash dishes or clothes, ran errands, and carried firewood or coal . . . In one place I worked for a woman who was newly married. She had been a laundry girl . . . earning [her own] money; but once married, her husband said no wife of his could work! He forced her out of her active, independent life into a three-room house where most of the work was done by me after school . . .

"After the first few weeks of Gladys' married life she and her husband began their quarrels. Neighboring women listened from behind drawn blinds. When she complained to them, as women beyond the tracks did, they all seemed to agree that a woman had to 'mind' her husband. Something within me revolted at this and I hated and despised them all."

Gladys longs to return to work, but the husband says over his dead body.

"So Gladys did not go back to work. Months passed and the neighbors smiled . . . for now it was said she was 'expectin'.' And the quarrels with her husband continued. The words that passed between them are still carved into my memory as if a dagger had made its ruthless way there.

" 'Give me back the clothes I bought you!' he bellowed at her one day.

" 'Damn it, kid, you know I love you!' she begged through her tears—for now she could not go back to work even if she wished.

"Two other women in the next yard heard the words through the window and they laughed. She couldn't be so uppish any more, they said. I did not laugh. There was something in the words so heart-corroding that I could not even repeat them at home; only once since in my life have I been able to repeat them, and that once when I was trying to find the source of my hatred of marriage and my disgust for women who are wives. Those two sentences sum up, in my mind, the true position of the husband and wife in the marriage relationship."

The unrelenting hardness of this voice is the distinguishing characteristic of *Daughter of Earth*. It is the voice of the girl who will cross Colorado, Oklahoma, and Arizona alone, forcing her way through cold, hunger, and danger with a gun hidden in her clothes, tearing at the men who come at her not the bears, making her way at last to New York City where, in the years before the First World War, she becomes a teacher, a journalist, and a partisan of revolutionary movements: all the while hugging to herself a hatred—of "the system" and of the despair of having been born a woman—that never qualifies itself, burning as brightly at the end as at the beginning. In her own words, "I am become a hard, thankless, graceless girl, and it was the only way I could do it." Herein lie the crude strength and obvious limitation in the voice of *Daughter of Earth*'s truth speaker. Not to mention the glaring avoidances.

What Smedley is never straight about is herself and sex. She is passionate, and she hates herself for it. Hating herself, she lashes out. Never once does she acknowledge the stir of sensuality within her own being. Instead, it is always a man (some animal) who is the cause of her recurrent "downfalls."

At nineteen she meets a man of advanced education—given to a utopian vision of love as partnership—who falls hard and begs her to marry him. She does, and, precisely because she is aroused by her husband, she begins to abuse him. The marriage fails. Later, in New York, she becomes a member of the Indian independence movement in exile. The men in the movement—Gandhi's early followers—welcome her with warmth, gratitude, and suspicion. In spite of herself Smedley is attracted to one among them, a handsome, sneering womanizer. When he comes after her, she, of course, succumbs—and then reviles him. The description of the seduction is startling because we see clearly her own collusion but hear only a diatribe against the Indian's baseness, his moral failure, his animal brutishness. Still later she marries the Nelson Mandela among the Indians—a soft, intelligent, upright man—and lies to him about her affair with his comrade (as well as all the others she has casually bedded down with by now). Again the marriage corrodes. Again Smedley fails to see how much her own anger and cunning contribute to the madness that overtakes her and her husband.

Yet she suffers—how she suffers!—over sex. The penalty and the allure are always there, twisting around inside her. The fear, the heat, the self-loathing—the inability to accept or forgo—is in itself an essence of persona in *Daughter of Earth*, and it is the making of the memoir. What saves the book from didacticism is precisely this nasty complication of the narrator's relation to herself. Closed, hard, defensive, she nonetheless lets us see it all, and the writing accumulates into a truth, of which the narrator's dishonesty with herself is a vital element.

What we have here is an American Gorky speaking: a tale of hatred and self-hatred being told in the style of an untutored oral history, its eloquence all the more powerful for its cunning and its lack of nuance. Obsessing over the all-too-simple elements of her unspeakable condition, Smedley has the power to suggest an abandonment of primeval proportions. If she were a greater writer, she would have been able to make class and sex deepen into a tale of original loss: unredeemable inner damage, Freudian and mythical. As it is, born into the company of those who will live and die exiled from *any* idea of the self, she has written a book that is a masterly evocation of what it *feels* like to be that disinherited creature, condemned to the singular loneliness of American individualism.

■   ■

From *Father and Son* to *Daughter of Earth* to *The Duke of Deception* is an education in the extraordinary progress across the last century of the memoir of "becoming." Written in the late 1970s, *The Duke of Deception* is a memoir whose author, Geoffrey Wolff, is neither a believer in an inviolable self in need of liberation nor a man struggling up out of poetic primitivism to insist only that he *has* an inviolable self. He is, rather, a man who sets out to document what the narrator of every work of twentieth-century literature has been at pains to demonstrate—that the task is to become acquainted with the stranger who lives inside your own skin, the one who answers when your name is called. Especially when called by your father, if you're a boy and he is the one you cleaved to from the moment you first drew breath, the one in whose image you think you have been made.

The Duke of Deception is a fine demonstration of what a male writer is up to when he sets out to write about his father as though about a psychological counterpart, and does it so well that from the opening description the intimate connection between the one speaking and the one being spoken of is made to seem emblematic:

"My father, called Duke, taught me skills and manners; he taught me to shoot and to drive fast and to read respectfully and to box and to handle a boat and to distinguish between good jazz music and bad jazz music . . . His codes were not novel, but they were rigid, the rules of decorum that Hemingway prescribed. A gentleman kept his word, and favored simplicity of sentiment; a gentleman chose his words with care, as he chose his friends. A gentleman accepted responsibility for his acts, and welcomed the liberty to act unambiguously. A gentleman was a stickler for precision and punctilio; life was no more than an inventory of small choices that together formed a man's character, entire. A gentleman was this, and not that; a *man* did, did not, said, would not say.

"My father could, however, be coaxed to reveal his bona fides. He had been schooled at Groton and passed along to Yale. He was just barely prepared to intimate that he had been tapped for 'Bones' and I remember his pleasure when Levi Jackson, the black captain of Yale's 1948 football team, was similarly honored by that secret

society. He was proud of Skull and Bones for its hospital-
ity toward the exotic. He did sometimes wince, however,
when he pronounced Jackson's Semitic Christian name,
and I sensed that his tolerance for Jews was not inclusive;
but I never heard him indulge express bigotry, and the first
of half a dozen times he hit me was for having called a
neighbor's kid a guinea . . .

"If Duke's preoccupation with bloodlines was finite,
this did not cause him to be unmindful of his ancestors.
He knew whence he had come, and whither he meant me
to go. I saw visible evidence of this, a gold signet ring
which I wear today, a heavy bit of business inscribed arsy-
turvy with lions and flora and a motto, *nulla vestigium
retrorsit*. 'Don't look back' I was told it meant.

"After Yale—class of late nineteen-twenty something
or early nineteen-thirty something—my father batted
around the country, living a high life in New York among
school and college chums, flying as a test pilot, marrying
my mother, the daughter of a rear admiral. I was born a
year after the marriage, in 1937, and three years after that
my father went to England as a fighter pilot with Eagle
Squadron, a group of American volunteers in the Royal
Air Force. Later, he transferred to the OSS and . . . just before the Invasion he was parachuted into Normandy . . .

"A pretty history for an American clubman. Its fault
is that it was not true. My father was a bullshit artist.
True, there were many boarding schools, each less pleased
with the little Duke than the last, but none of them was
Groton. There was no Yale, and by the time he walked

from a room at a mention of Skull and Bones I knew this, and he knew that I knew it. No military service would have him; his teeth were bad. So he had his teeth pulled and replaced, but the Air Corps and Navy and Army and Coast Guard still thought he was a bad idea. The ring I wear was made according to his instructions by a jeweler two blocks from Schwab's drugstore in Hollywood, and was never paid for. The motto, engraved backwards so that it would come right on a red wax seal, is dog Latin and means in fact 'leave no trace behind,' but my father did not believe me when I told him this.

"My father was a Jew. This did not seem to him a good idea, and so it was his notion to dissemble his history, begin at zero, and re-create himself. His sustaining line of work till shortly before he died was as a confidence man. If I now find his authentic history more surprising, more interesting, than his counterfeit history, he did not. He would not make his peace with his actualities, and so he was the author of his own circumstances, and indifferent to the consequences of this nervy program . . . There were some awful consequences, for other people as well as for him."

Arthur Wolff was born in 1907 in Hartford, Connecticut, the son of a rich, middle-class doctor. He grew up warm, intelligent, spoiled; and somewhere along the way some awful piece of damage got put in place that made him a man permanently at odds with the very *idea* of doing the world by the world's rules. That is, of earning his way. Having the best because he had paid for the best.

Resistance to earning our way is the common lot of humanity—we all resent *deeply* having to grow up—but one way or another, most of us make our peace with the requirement short of criminal recalcitrance. Arthur Wolff could not. The compulsion never to bring himself under discipline ruled his psyche. There was, finally, nothing and no one that could more command his loyalty. The need to have the best, and not pay for it, determined every move he made until the day he died.

It was a life of taking jobs he lied his way into; buying cars, clothes, gadgets he would never actually purchase; being perpetually flush or broke; leaving a house or a hotel or a state in the middle of the night. And throughout his buoyant, daring youth, landing royally on his feet. Some marvelous mixture of the warmth, intelligence, and talent that was his by nature mingled well for many years with the mad courage of his deranged brashness; together, they converted into *genuine* fakery. Repeatedly "he was fired by companies fed up with his debts, his arrogance, or his insubordination; he was never fired for incompetence."

The mixture—the giftedness, the mad hungers, the emotional ruthlessness—proved erotic in its ability to compel the inner attention of the boy growing in its aura: provided an injection into the nervous system of excitement and anxiety that nothing could prevent from becoming formative. This complication of attraction-repulsion riddles the book, is laced through the prose, coloring every anecdote and turn of event, every surging bit of promise and sick-making disappointment.

The goodness of *The Duke of Deception* turns—as it does in *Father and Son*—on the rich, full gaze that the narrating son levels at the emotional extravagance of the singular parent. Here, too, we have a tale of growing up under the influence of a man in the grip of his own psychological addictions—being a scam artist is as driven an act for Arthur Wolff as praying five times a day is for Philip Gosse—and here, too, we see that influence become the royal road *in* for the man who is remembering. But the genius of this memoir lies in its letting us see how much the narrator *becomes* his father rather than struggles to separate from his father.

From earliest age, Geoffrey, too, apes the look and style of the rich and the socially connected. Very young, he, too, knows the name of everything—boats, cars, schools; wine, clothing, tennis rackets—and he, too, loves faking it, loves getting something (everything) for nothing. He also feels the raging emptiness that follows hard upon the single-minded pursuit of instant gratification—the thing that is wanted now, right now, cost be damned. The single-mindedness is chilling; and so is the emptiness.

When Geoffrey was ten years old, "I loved the trashman's daughter, Margaret, and she did not love me back . . . [She] was tall, intelligent, dignified, reserved . . . I dreamt of having her in our house for dinner, and keeping her there, forever . . .

"Duke listened to me tell about Margaret Dean, and advised me well . . . And like everyone who asks advice about love, I didn't follow my father's. I assaulted Margaret with unsigned notes, and then with signed notes declaring love. I ruined her days in school. Once she brushed past me walking to lunch and said one word: 'Please.' I mistook her meaning, and glowed all day. That night I telephoned . . . She hung up when I stammered my name. I sent her a note:

" 'Yesterday you said please to me. I love you.'

"And a note, for once, came back: 'I meant please leave me alone. I don't like you.'

". . . [T]he Christmas of our fifth-grade year I developed a plan. I was given my usual twenty-five dollars to shop . . . This year I bought my mother nothing, my father and brother nothing. It seemed to me my plan could not fail to win me Margaret Dean. The plan hinged upon giving two gifts, one of them commonplace, the other a *coup d'éclat*. The first was a gift to my beloved of wool mittens [that cost two dollars] . . . I was left with twenty-three dollars, and I spent it all on a [top-of-the-line] chemistry set . . . This gift was not for me, nor for anyone in my class, nor for anyone with whom I had ever exchanged a word. It was for the nicest boy in the sixth grade, the best looking, best athlete, most popular—Walter 'Walky' Dean.

"On the last day of school before Christmas, during the class party, I gave Margaret her mittens, and without reading the card . . . without opening the package . . . she dropped the gift in a rubbish bin. I was hurt, but not surprised. I walked across the hall to Mrs. Graves's sixth-grade classroom. I set the heavy, lavishly wrapped box on the desk of Walter Dean and said, 'Here. I love your sister. Make her love me back.' "

On Christmas morning, "they let me at the stuff before dawn, and watched me. It was grotesque, I think. I loved it, tearing at a sixth package before I had finished unwrapping a fifth." Among the presents is a chemistry set. "I got just what I had given [Walky Dean]; my father was trying to tell me something, or make me feel better. I also got a Flexible Flyer, and that morning, riding it down icy Braggart's Hill I set my tongue against the metal steering bar, and it stuck; when I tore my tongue away it bled so badly that I had to be taken to Dr. Von Glaun."

Years later, this incident is weirdly echoed. An unhappy preppie at Choate, Geoffrey meets and falls in love with a girl from Philadelphia: "She liked me, for a while, and visited me for a day and night in Wilton during her Christmas vacation. I had hoped she would stay longer, but she lost interest quickly . . . [and asked to be taken to the train].

"That night I wrote her a letter, twenty or thirty pages, maybe fifty. Falsehood on falsehood . . . References to my upcoming social season, so busy with coming-out parties in Boston and New York. The summer looked full too, Pater would be off as usual doing polo . . . I'd be playing the eastern tennis circuit . . . I wrote it on Raquet Club stationery my father had cadged . . . and I know I sealed the envelope with wax from a Christmas candle and stuck Duke's crest . . . in the wax.

". . . [M]y father found the letter, opened it, read it.

He didn't bring it to me. He destroyed it first, and then came to my room and woke me. He knew the toll, to the penny; he was so gentle. He didn't quote the letter at me, or refer to it. He told me I was better than I thought, that I didn't need to add to my sum. I had warmth, he said; warmth and energy were the important things. These were a long time paying off sometimes, but they paid off. Honesty was the crucial thing, he said, knowing who I was, being who I was. What he said was so; I knew it was so. I didn't even think to turn his words against him, he was trying so hard to save me from something, turn me back. I had this from him always: compassion, care, generosity, endurance."

In the end, Geoffrey becomes both more and less than his father. More in that he accepts the strength of finite reality: we are what we do. Less in that he closes down on the peculiar poetry of that which cannot *bear* to live only with what is earned. It is the considerable accomplishment of *The Duke of Deception* that this distinction is embedded in the texture of its prose: never lost sight of, never shortchanged.

In 1907 Edmund Gosse thought he had to leave his father to become himself; seventy years later Geoffrey Wolff knows he cannot leave his father because he has become his father. Agnes Smedley also knows what the century knows: that we become what is done to us. Not only is there no fixed nature within waiting to be freed up; the effort at liberation is in itself profoundly compromised.

In Edmund Gosse, Agnes Smedley, Geoffrey Wolff, we

have a set of memoirists whose work records a steadily changing idea of the emergent self. But for each of them a flash of insight illuminating that idea grew out of the struggle to clarify one's own formative experience; and in each case the strength and beauty of the writing lie in the power of concentration with which this insight is pursued, and made to become the writer's organizing principle. That principle at work is what makes a memoir literature rather than testament.

■　　■

Having said that the narrator in a memoir must always be reliable, always working hard to get to the bottom of the experience in hand, let me now turn to a pair of memoirists who complicate truth speaking prodigiously. Two of the most neurotic narrators in the annals of memoir writing are Oscar Wilde and Thomas De Quincey, a pair of feverish confessors much invested in recording the negative activity of the *un*-emerging self— the self permanently trapped, as William James once said, in "one long contradiction between knowledge and action"—and do it so magnificently that the reader is left in each instance with an unforgettable demonstration of how it is exactly that people cannot make use of the gifts with which they are born.

The voice speaking in *De Profundis* is akin to that of the modern analysand who repeats, desperately and with increasing brilliance (as though salvation lies in the talent of his description), a set of insights the analyst soon realizes will never be acted upon. The voice in *Confessions of an English Opium-Eater* relates a self-incriminating tale of "life, true life," written by a man who works hard at not seeing himself clearly. Both are compulsive talkers, both have pained histories to "explain," and both are driven to reveal themselves as men whose egregious sufferings are easily traced to a will permanently divided against itself. Ordinarily, such narrators would arouse only suspicion and distrust. Yet here the very single-mindedness with which each narrator lets us see what he himself cannot see becomes a form of reliability—one that speaks truth, not directly, to be sure, but truth nonetheless.

Thomas De Quincey was born in Manchester in 1785 into a prosperous and orderly family where he was neither neglected nor oppressed. In fact—as he was handsome, charming, and intellectually gifted—everyone he met was much taken with him. Yet from earliest life he was afflicted with an unabating sense of worthlessness that no external experience could bring under control; always he felt that he was despised and on the verge of abandonment. These feelings induced in him a volatility that could not sustain a moment's frustration: he was forever bolting. At seventeen—the brightest boy in the class by far, and obviously headed for a fine university career—De Quincey ran away from school, made his way to Wales and then to London, where he ended up broke, hungry, and homeless, living on the street in the derelict company that clearly mirrored his deepest inner feeling. What he needed, always, was relief:

from himself. The minute he tasted opium—in 1804 at the age of eighteen—he was home free. At first he took it only occasionally, but by 1812 he was taking it once a week, the year after that daily. The rest of his life was one long, self-reviling negotiation with the drug.

Oscar Wilde was also wellborn and well loved, and he, too, was formed by an anxiety of the self that ruled him in ways far better papered over, for far longer, than De Quincey was able to manage. But self-hatred was not to be denied. In 1895, at the age of forty, Wilde was a famous man: famous, rich, internationally celebrated. That year he met Alfred Douglas and fell desperately in love. The affair was obsessive, and it was nasty: public scenes, low-life amusements, voyeuristic sex. The two were mismatched in every way except the only one that mattered: each one touched in the other the secret sense of unworthiness to which both were devoted. Each became the instrument of downfall the other craved. Nothing but scandal and prison could separate them. And, as it turned out, not even that.

Both Wilde and De Quincey write in the confiding style of a man about to describe that which is behind him. Each one readily persuades the reader that he honestly believes that to speak the truth *now* is to free himself. De Quincey tells us at the outset that he has suffered unjustly from being reputed to have brought upon himself all the sufferings that he now must record; he wants to explain to us that he first used the drug only to mitigate a stomach pain of the severest sort, and because the youthful experiences that produced this pain were interesting in themselves, he will here briefly retrace them, and we will see for ourselves how entirely understandable it is that he came to be where he has been. *De Profundis*, a ninety-page letter that Wilde sent to Alfred Douglas in the last months of his incarceration at Reading Gaol, is, in its turn, a piece written by a man who needs to believe that he has achieved overview and is now in a position to put into significant perspective the harrowing history of the tragedy he realizes he has helped bring about.

De Profundis is remarkable for the speed and efficiency with which Wilde states the case and establishes a believable atmosphere of introspection, one in which we feel him doggedly trying to see things as they are, be just, bring insight and accusation into line, recognize his own part in what has transpired. In the first thirty pages he gives a dazzling account of the struggle within:

"The real fool, such as the gods mock or mar, is he who does not know himself. I was such a one too long. You have been such a one too long. Be so no more . . . The supreme vice is shallowness. Everything that is realised is right . . .

" . . . As I sit here in this dark cell in convict clothes, a disgraced and ruined man, I blame myself. In the perturbed and fitful nights of anguish, in the long monotonous days of pain, it is myself I blame . . . for allowing an unintellectual friendship . . . entirely to dominate my life . . .

"Of the appalling results of my friendship with you I don't speak at present. I am thinking merely of its quality while it lasted. It was intellectually degrading to me . . . Your interests were merely in your meals and moods. Your desires were simply for amusements . . . I blame myself without reserve for my weakness. It was merely weakness . . . But in the case of an artist, weakness is nothing less than a crime, when it is a weakness that paralyses the imagination . . .

". . . You demanded without grace and received without thanks. You grew to think that you had a sort of right to live at my expense and in a profuse luxury to which you had never been accustomed . . . Out of the reckless dinners with you nothing remains but the memory that too much was eaten and too much was drunk. And my yielding to your demands was bad for you . . . It made you grasping . . . unscrupulous . . . ungracious . . .

". . . I had always thought that my giving up to you in small things meant nothing: that when a great moment arrived I could myself re-assert my will power in its natural superiority. It was not so. At the great moment my will power completely failed me. In life there is really no great or small thing. All things are of equal value and of equal size. My habit of giving up to you in everything had become insensibly a real part of my nature . . .

"Ultimately the bond of all companionship, whether in marriage or in friendship, is conversation, and conversation must have a common basis, and between two people of widely different culture the only common basis possible is the lowest level . . . [I]t was only in the mire that we met . . .

"I must say to myself that I ruined myself, and that nobody great or small can be ruined except by his own hand . . . Terrible as was what the world did to me, what I did to myself is far more terrible still . . . I became the spendthrift of my own genius . . . I took pleasure where it pleased me, and passed on. I forgot that every little action of the common day makes or unmakes character, and that therefore what one has done in the secret chamber one has someday to cry aloud on the house-tops . . .

"I want to get to the point when I shall be able to say quite simply, and without affectation, that the two great turning-points in my life were when my father sent me to Oxford, and when Society sent me to prison . . .

"The supreme vice is shallowness. Whatever is realised is right . . .

"To deny one's own experience is to put a lie into the lips of one's own life. It is no less than a denial of the soul."

All this and more Wilde says in thirty admirably impassioned pages, pages that let him do and be everything: eloquent, farsighted, stoic. He sees it all, understands it all, says it all.

And then he says it all again.

And yet again.

The whole performance is given three times, the entire mixture of insight, accusation, and *mea culpa* tumbling together in no particular order. The writing continues to dazzle while the structure falls apart. And rightly so. Because, after all, what difference does it really make—the second and third times around—which comes first? We are in the presence of a man in a trance of self-analysis: a man who will never act on what he knows and therefore is compelled to go on "knowing."

Yet the piece is undeniably powerful. We are moved rather than put off by the stunning exhibition of human incapacity. Wilde's performance mimics the anguish of compulsive repetition—the intelligence quivers, the rhetoric dignifies—reproducing full strength the stranglehold of insight in a vacuum. Ineluctably the scope narrows down. The writing itself becomes the equivalent of a life in thrall.

De Quincey's speaking voice is even more open and confiding than Wilde's, and we fall in easily with his wonderfully reasonable account of his own early life: how he came to arrive at the place in which he now finds himself. We sense that the narrator may be rationalizing, but the voice is so focused, so intent, so assured that we are carried right along. Yet, beneath the unbroken flow of its rhetoric, somehow a note of doom has been sounding—as in a tale of unavoidable fate—so that a third of the way into the *Confessions*, when the narrator says, "It is so long since I first took opium, that if it had been a trifling incident in my life, I might have forgotten its date: but cardinal events are not to be forgotten," we find ourselves stopped in place, struck, even pained, by the sentence. The man speaking seems suddenly like a narrator in Poe, one destined to sink into a black night of the soul, drowning in full sight of respectable society: "alone, alone, alone." He cannot reach us, we cannot reach him; he can only call out from the solitary space on which he stands.

It's the solitariness that is so striking. Throughout all his adventures—leaving school, going broke, dropping without halt into the life of the streets—throughout it all De Quincey seems dramatically alone. Not another human being is ever called into life: all are skeletal; all stand in shadow. Of his family, not a word; they seem never to have existed. We are listening to a man who's been living alone inside his head forever; and his head is a place of disorder wherein no companion is to be found, a place he himself cannot bear yet cannot leave. How can anyone else be invited to visit this chaos?

But wait. There is hope. There is promise. There is opium.

"The pleasure given by wine is . . . acute—[that given by opium] chronic . . . the one is a flame, the other a steady and equable glow. But the main distinction lies in this, that whereas wine disorders the mental faculties, opium, on the contrary, . . . introduces amongst them the most exquisite order, legislation, and harmony. Wine robs a man of his self-possession: opium greatly invigorates it. Wine unsettles and clouds the judgement, and gives a preternatural brightness, and a vivid exaltation to the contempts and the admirations, the loves and the hatreds, of

the drinker: opium, on the contrary, communicates serenity and equipoise to all the faculties, active or passive . . .
Wine constantly leads a man to the brink of absurdity and
extravagance; and, beyond a certain point, it is sure to
volatilize and to disperse the intellectual energies: whereas
opium always seems to compose what had been agitated,
and to concentrate what had been distracted. In short . . .
the opium-eater . . . feels that . . . the diviner part of his
nature is paramount; that is, the moral affections are in a
state of cloudless serenity; and over all is the great light of
the majestic intellect . . . This is the doctrine of the true
church on the subject of opium: of which church I acknowledge myself to be the only member—the alpha and
the omega."

Listen to what the narrator is telling us. He takes
opium to be not less responsible but more responsible, not
to bliss out but to clear out. He takes it to wake in a state
of peace sufficient for coherent thought. All he wants is
to live decently inside his own mind. That, and nothing
more.

From the moment we read this description of the joys
of opium, we know something about De Quincey that he
himself is not willing to know: that the deal he is cutting is
Faustian in nature. It will end with him in an isolation of
even more horrifying proportion than that which he now
endures. And so it transpires. Inevitably, the promise of
opium turns in on itself, and the piper is there waiting to
be paid:

"My studies have now been long interrupted. I cannot read to myself with any pleasure, hardly with a moment's endurance . . . The sublimer and more passionate poets I still read . . . But my proper vocation, as I well knew, was the exercise of the analytic understanding. Now, for the most part, analytic studies are continuous, and not to be pursued by fits and starts, or fragmentary efforts. Mathematics, for instance, intellectual philosophy, & c. were all become insupportable to me. I shrunk from them with a sense of powerless and infantine feebleness that gave me an anguish the greater from remembering the time when I grappled with them to my own hourly delight."

At the last, having mustered a final intellectual enthusiasm for political economy, and wanting to publish thoughts on the subject he has already committed to paper, he cannot even complete a preface and a dedication.

By now, of course, the dreams—the gorgeous and terrible dreams for which the *Confessions* is famous—have overtaken his nights. He lives in a continuous state of exhaustion. Night after night after night, the astonishing spectacles unfold in his sleep, moving relentlessly from the vivid and the beautiful to the grotesque and the overwhelming, giving way in serial form from one elemental setting to another until at last we arrive at those embedded in water:

"The waters now changed their character—from translucent lakes, shining like mirrors, they now became seas and oceans . . . Hitherto the human face had mixed often in my dreams, but not despotically, nor with any special power of tormenting. But now . . . upon the rocking waters of the ocean the human face began to appear: the sea appeared paved with innumerable faces, upturned to the heavens: faces, imploring, wrathful, despairing, surged upwards by the thousands, by myriads, by generations, by centuries—my agitation was infinite—my mind tossed—and surged with the ocean."

Who, after Freud, would ever again have such dreams?

De Quincey lived thirty years beyond the writing of the *Confessions*. He took opium until the day he died. His was the despair of the man driven to undo himself: the man who will never pull it together; the man who burrows compulsively back into a sense of abandonment that originates in the cradle. That burrowing is the source of the divided will: the will that both wants and at the same time does not want to cohere, emerge, become.

Confessions of an English Opium-Eater is a remarkable piece of self-observation. Like *De Profundis*, it is a record of neurotic stasis that escapes the charge of obsessional writing only by becoming, very nearly, the thing itself: a concentrate of inner exile, an essence of self-defeat.

De Quincey's was the solitariness of a soul unable to make a connection with another because it could not connect with itself. A theme to be continued well into the next century, when some of the best memoirs written were organized out of an underlying recognition of the true nature of loneliness and narrated by men and women able to speak what they know only obliquely.

■　　　■

Man is himself, like the universe he inhabits,
. . . a tale of desolation.

Loren Eiseley spent forty years as an anthropologist looking at bones, animals, and oceans, with an instinctive sense of metaphor applied to all his findings. His writing is memorable for the singular detachment he brings to large, poetic evocations of geologic time, unearthed civilizations, the evolutionary nature of all that lives. In his essays Eiseley is a voyager steering a narrow course that widens steadily into a largeness of consideration by no means always sanguine. The gaze of the man behind the words, however, is calm, open, unagitated—resolved upon integrating whatever comes into view. So successful is the merger between narrator and subject in these essays about the world—with or without dinosaurs, or flowers, or starfish—that any reader might justifiably conclude that the writer is himself a man long emerged from his own chaos, now working in a state of inner equilibrium.

The tone of the essays is the tone Eiseley meant to apply to the memoir he completed shortly before his death in 1977. He intended that this book, *All the Strange Hours*, would present its protagonist not intimately but within a scope of consideration similar to the one he had applied all his working life. He would treat himself much as he would any other specimen he might dig out (in fact, the memoir is subtitled *The Excavation of a Life*). We were to view him as a kind of prototypical being alive on the planet at this time, in this place. The book he actually wrote is remarkable because the writing welled up out of a place beyond the reach of conscious intent and it rescued him repeatedly from his own defensiveness.

Eiseley was born in 1907 in Nebraska. His father was a decent man who read books and seemed to fail at almost everything he tried. His mother was profoundly deaf and had once been beautiful; deafness and anger led her to become a creature of guttural sound, wary and at bay. Their presence was lonely-making. Within himself, the boy turned away to the glorious emptiness before him, to the birds and animals, the fossils and desert striations he found out on the sunbaked Nebraska plain. Here, in this silence, he did not feel alone.

The father died; there was no money; Loren dropped out of school, left home at nineteen, and began to wander. "All over America men were drifting like sargasso weed in a vast dead sea of ruined industry," among them the young Loren Eiseley. The Depression suited him fine. Riding the rails, surviving in hobo encampments, enduring the brutishness of a world hung with the sign JOBLESS MEN KEEP GOING—all this confirmed him (even then) in his belief that "there is nothing more alone in the universe than man . . . [Only] in rare and hidden moments of communion with nature, does man briefly escape his solitary destiny."

In his late twenties Eiseley broke out of the long cycle of poverty and wandering, returned to school, became an anthropologist with a strong talent for writing, went on to graduate school and a life in teaching and university administration. He wrote many books of essays and poetry, all meant to "excavate" the relationship between man and the animals, man and the elements, man and the universe, man and anything but people. Throughout his life Eiseley experienced himself as a solitary. It matters not that he was, in fact, married, with friends, colleagues, and students in abundance; it matters only that this is how he saw himself: a man alone among men. As the years went on and the books piled up, he became persuaded that he had been destined for the company of the universe, not of human fellowship—and that was fine, just fine. When he sat down to write his memoir, he considered himself both knowing and at peace on that score. Yet the prose, almost from the start, strikes a note distinctly at odds with that measured consideration.

Not more than twenty pages in, Eiseley casually describes his mother as "paranoid, neurotic and unstable"—terms of description unalarming to the reader of modern memoir—but then, in an unexpected outburst, he writes:

"There will be those to say in this mother-worshipping culture that I am harsh, embittered. They will be quite wrong. Why should I be embittered? It is far too late. A month ago, after a passage of many years, I stood above her grave . . . We, she and I, were close to being one now, lying like the skeletons of last year's leaves in a fence corner. And it was all nothing. Nothing, do you understand? All the pain, all the anguish. Nothing. We were, both of us, merely the debris life always leaves in its passing, like the maimed discarded chicks in a hatchery tray—no more than that. For a little longer I would see and hear, but it was nothing, and to the world it would mean nothing."

The passage is startling. The directness jars. The directness and the nakedness. It's the "Nothing, do you understand?" that does it. In that quivering insistence we feel the presence of a seventy-year-old man whose thin skin is still stretched across an open wound.

A few pages later Eiseley describes a dinner with W. H. Auden, an admirer of his work. The dinner goes badly. By his own admission, he has been feeling uncomfortable with the great poet, diminished somehow in his presence. Auden, aware of the stiffness between them, is chatting to set them at ease. He asks Eiseley, who is exactly his age, to name the earliest public event he remembers, and mentions, briefly, that in his case it was the sinking of the *Titanic* in 1912. Eiseley replies by falling into an extended reverie over a prison break (also in 1912) that took place near his home, letting his voice go self-consciously "poetic" as he speaks ("He blew the gates with nitroglycerin. I was five years old . . . already old enough to know one should flee from the universe but I did not know where to run . . . There was an armed posse and a death . . . We never made it"). The tale is long, self-dramatizing, and unmistakably competitive. Yet we are touched, not embarrassed, by it because we've already been given a taste of the rawness inside the man.

To a considerable degree, the entire book is an ever-deepening clarification of these two passages, each in its own way harrowing: the one a transparent denial of pain everlasting, the other of a longing akin to the pain that dare not be addressed openly. Chapter headings may read "The Rat That Danced," or "Toads and Men," or "The Coming of the Giant Wasps," but we are engaged by the man who told us more than he meant to tell himself when he rapped out "Nothing, do you understand?" and then related the story of his dinner with Auden. What that man is grappling with is the experience this memoir is wanting to shape.

It is in the chapters on the wandering years that we first meet the man who identifies with nature, not with people, and feel the weight and consequence of his grievance. In some of the best Depression writing you will ever read, Eiseley evokes the despairing antagonism of the time: a kind of starved, murderous haze that keeps drifting up from the middle of the socialized world.

Once during this period a vicious brakeman tries to push him off a moving train. "He struck me across the face and pushed," Eiseley writes. "A thin hot wire like that in an incandescent lamp began to flicker in my brain . . . 'Kill him, kill him,' blazed the red wire. 'He's trying to kill you.' " Hours later, in a hobo camp, he is asked about his swollen face. When Eiseley explains, the man who questioned him (as though taking his cue from Steinbeck) says, "Just get this straight. The capitalists beat men into line. Okay? The communists beat men into line. Right again? . . . Men beat men, that's all. That's all there is. Remember it, kid." Of this exchange Eiseley remarks with some irony, "That man, whose name I never knew, . . . left all my life henceforward free of mobs and movements, free as only very wild things are both solitary and free." But the real conclusion of the story comes when Eiseley observes of himself that often, over the years, in trying to tell what he knows, he has felt that "the tale I had intended . . . had been lost in the incoherence of a split personality, the murderer who had not murdered but who carried a red wire glowing in his brain."

Of this man—the civilized writer with the red wire still glowing in his brain—he speaks rarely and only indirectly. The indirection leads him into dark waters: "Men should discover their past. I admit to this. It has been my profession. Only so can we learn our limitations and come in time to suffer life with compassion. Nevertheless, I now believe there are occasions when . . . to tamper with the past, even one's own, is to bring [on] that slipping, sliding horror which revolves around all that is done, unalterable, and yet which abides unseen in the living mind . . . [and makes] us lonely beyond belief."

He is speaking here of the unexpected consequences of one or two world-famous excavations, but of course that is not what he is speaking of at all. This far I go, the writing says. No further.

As Eiseley draws close to the present, it seems suddenly to matter that he has never known human intimacy. At his mother's funeral he pleads inarticulately with his wife of forty years—a woman to whom he refers three times in passing, and only once by name—to assure him that they have indeed lived their life. She does as she's asked, but her words are of no use to him. Anxiety now drives the language on, making it swell to allegorical proportions: there are talking cats, giant wasps, mythical struggles in a blinding, primeval snow.

Abruptly he pulls himself together. In a satchel his mother left him, he finds a huge forgotten bone from his early diggings, an Ice Age bison forelimb that sits now on his desk. He lifts the bone, meditates on it, and, at the very last, tells us that whatever the conflicts have been about, this much he knows: "I did not care for taxonomic definitions, that was the truth of it. I did not care to be a man, only a being."

The sentence is a cry from the heart, one that resonates in the reader. We have spent the last three hundred pages in the company of a man whose attempt to "excavate" the human awfulness behind that sentence has been valiant. Now he falls back exhausted, telling us, "Dig as I may, I cannot get directly at it"; and we are moved because we have experienced the depth of his effort. It's the effort that makes him a trustworthy narrator.

Loren Eiseley was a man who opened his eyes nearly every morning of his life into a vast and etherizing depression. It was his inclination—as it is everyone's inclination—to make of his own disability a universal truth ("a tale of desolations," indeed). Yet every morning he also swung his legs over the side of the bed, stood up, walked across the room, sat down at his desk, and began to work. The act alone steadied him, helped him resist self-dramatization. Eiseley *wants* to romanticize his own solitary state—define existence itself as loneliness incarnate—but somewhere within himself—and this is the thing he cannot look directly at—he knows that the isolation is self-created. In this memoir the working habit he has developed of naming the thing accurately struggles with the need to poeticize what he can barely acknowledge. The struggle characterizes his persona, the narrator whose singular speaking voice gives *All the Strange Hours* both its integrity and its haunting quality.

■   ■

Eiseley's memoir is emblematic of a preoccupation with human isolation that has been growing steadily over the past hundred years—and the problem it has presented memoir writing. When that preoccupation surfaces through a first-person narrator in modernist fiction, the reader instantly feels the open artifice of the speaking voice—"I am alone. I have always been alone. Alone is what I am"—and just as instantly accepts it as authentic. It's a deeply familiar sound, that voice. From Dostoyevsky to Beckett, it delivers the message of the century through the felt power of a truth-speaking fiction.

In nonfiction, of course, such artifice is unacceptable. The narrator would be experienced as an embarrassment, a naïf, a creature foolishly self-dramatizing. No, in memoir "alone again" will never do. In fact, exactly the opposite is required. If the solitude of self is the real subject, memoirists generally do better when they speak through the filter of that which passes for a subject well beyond themselves: a solution derived from the hard-won understanding that to speak otherwise is to risk ending in rhetoric or abstraction. Such memoirs often adopt a posture through the narrating persona akin to that of the literary journalist: "I am only here reporting on a piece of the world enterprise. Myself, that is not what this is about." When, in fact, "myself" is precisely what this is about.

Three distinctive memoirs, written across a span of fifty-odd years, strike me as admirably representative of this eminently practical approach to an otherwise intractable writing problem: Beryl Markham's *West with the Night* (1942), Marguerite Duras's *The Lover* (1984), and W. G. Sebald's *The Rings of Saturn* (1995). The first is a reminiscence of Africa, the second of sexual initiation, the third of a walking tour of the east coast of England. In these books, as the persona is not a confiding one, tone is everything. The first is grounded in a dignifying remoteness; the second is drenched in anomie; the third achieves religious calm. No matter. Each is marked powerfully by an apprehension of human solitariness expressed so richly and so peculiarly that *it* becomes the persona through which the memoirist speaks.

Beryl Markham was taken to Kenya in 1906, when she was four years old, by her father, one of the Brits in Africa who were more like T. E. Lawrence than Lord Mountbatten. Intelligent, passionate, physically fearless, these men and women could ride and hunt with a skill amounting to genius, and often they became mystical about Africa. Yet they shared the prejudices of their class and race—they might go native, but rarely did they go anti-imperialist—and while Africa liberated their senses, it did not encourage in them the value of human connection. Many of these people remained tempestuous spirits, coldly immature, devoted to adventure in the wilderness sense of that word. They loved Africa because Africa had given them the best of themselves, and love of Africa remains the best thing about them. Certainly, it is the best thing about Beryl Markham.

Africa, she tells us, "was the breath and life of my childhood. It is still the host of all my darkest fears, the cradle of mysteries always intriguing, but never wholly solved . . . It is as ruthless as any sea, more uncompromising than its own deserts . . . without temperance in its harshness or in its favours. It yields nothing, offering much to men of all races . . . But the soul of Africa, its integrity, the slow inexorable pulse of its life, is its own and of such singular rhythm that no outsider, unless steeped from childhood in its endless, even beat, can ever hope to experience it, except only as a bystander might experience a Masai war dance knowing nothing of its music nor the meaning of its steps."

With these words, Markham enters so wholly into the living memory of Africa—the animals, the natives, the land itself—that when she describes a horse or a dog feeling proud or lively or depressed, or a native hunter outwitting a lion, or a volcanic lake with a hundred thousand flamingos lighting down on it, we feel ourselves in the presence of a temperament so perfectly suited to its environment that we know, almost immediately the book begins, the use it makes of "Africa" will penetrate to a place well below the surface of the prose.

Her father had a gift for handling animals that he passed on to his daughter, a strong-willed, long-legged wild child always more at home with horses than with people. Horses, and later airplanes and danger. In 1930 Markham learned to fly, and between 1931 and 1935 she worked as an African bush pilot, delivering mail and passengers and spotting elephant for white hunters (among them, the men in Isak Dinesen's life, Bror Blixen and Denys Finch Hatton). In 1936 she became the first person to fly solo across the Atlantic east to west, from London to Nova Scotia. Throughout the 1940s she lived on her celebrity in London and California. In the 1950s she returned home, where she became a horse trainer on a grand scale, training many Derby winners over the next ten or fifteen years. She was married and divorced three times. She died in Nairobi in 1986, back in the only Africa she knew, where the vital connection was with animals, not with people. Animals and planes. The two elementals for this cold, beautiful danger-seeking woman who could find ease within herself nowhere on earth. Here she is describing the delivery from England of a studhorse she will come to love:

"He arrived in the early morning, descending the ramp from the noisy little train with the slow step of a royal exile. He held his head above the heads of those who led him, and smelled the alien earth and the thin air of the Highlands. It was not a smell that he knew.

"There was a star of white on his forehead; his nostrils were wide and showed crimson like the lacquered nostrils of a Chinese dragon. He was tall, deep in girth, slender-chested, on strong legs clean as marble.

"He was not chestnut; he was neither brown nor sorrel. He stood uncertainly against the foreign background—a rangy bay stallion swathed in sunlight and in a sheen of reddish gold.

"He knew that this was freedom again. He knew that the darkness and the terrifying movement of the ship that strained his legs and bruised his body against walls too close together were gone now.

"The net of leather rested on his head in those same places, and the long lines that he had learned to follow hung from the thing in his mouth that could not be bitten. But these he was used to. He could breathe, and he could feel the spring of the earth under his hooves. He could shake his body, and he could see that there was distance here, and a breadth of land into which he fitted. He opened his nostrils and smelled the heat and the emptiness of Africa and filled his lungs and let the rush of air go out of them again in a low, undulant murmur."

And here she is on the plane:

"There is a feeling of absolute finality about the end of a flight through darkness. The whole scheme of things with which you have lived acutely, during hours of roaring sound in an element altogether detached from the world, ceases abruptly. The plane noses groundward, the wings strain to the firmer cushion of earthbound air, wheels touch, and the engine sighs into silence. The dream of flight is suddenly gone before the mundane realities of growing grass and swirling dust, the slow plodding of men and the enduring patience of rooted trees. Freedom escapes you again, and wings that were a moment ago no less than an eagle's, and swifter, are metal and wood once more, inert and heavy . . .

"I climb out of the cockpit and watch a band of dim figures approach before the dancing flares . . . Somewhere an ancient automobile engine roared into life, its worn pistons and bearings hammering like drumbeats. Hot night wind stalked through the thorn leaves and leleshwa that surround the clearing. It bore the odour of swampland, the smell of Lake Victoria, the breath of weeds and sultry plains and tangled bush. It whipped at the oil flares and snatched at the surfaces of the [plane]. But there was loneliness in it and aimlessness, as if its passing were only a sterile duty lacking even the beneficent promise of rain."

These passages are moving evocations of an inner remoteness threaded through the entire narrative, and made all the more moving by virtue, on the one hand, of its open identification with the horse and, on the other, of its freedom from judgment of a world at whose edge she so awkwardly stands. Up in the plane the narrator is relieved of her alien condition; coming down she is plunged back into it. Yet she touches the ground and she does not hold the world in contempt; she has pity for it: the loneliness and the aimlessness. We are in the presence of high-minded detachment.

The voice that is holding all this together is a complex of the conventions of class and the surprise of temperament. It is the voice of someone who values decorum (would never dream of speaking confessionally), honors a code of behavior that calls for bearing the wounds of life in silence, and sees the pursuit of adventure as a test of valor. Yet accumulating beneath the surface of this exceptionally adaptive insularity is an emotional intelligence not at all hidden from itself, one that grows increasingly thoughtful, moving steadily toward an open understanding of what lies beneath the need for impenetrable self-protection:

"You can live a lifetime and, at the end of it, know more about other people than you know about yourself. You learn to watch other people, but you never watch yourself because you strive against loneliness. If you read a book, or shuffle a deck of cards, or care for a dog, you are avoiding yourself. The abhorrence of loneliness is as natural as wanting to live at all. If it were otherwise, men would never have bothered to make an alphabet, nor to have fashioned words out of what were only animal sounds, nor to have crossed continents—each man to see what the other looked like.

"Being alone in an aeroplane for even so short a time as a night and a day, irrevocably alone, with nothing to observe but your instruments and your own hands in semi-darkness, nothing to contemplate but the size of your small courage, nothing to wonder about but the beliefs, the faces, and the hopes rooted in your mind—such an experience can be as startling as the first awareness of a stranger walking by your side at night. You are the stranger."

At last we register how often the word "loneliness" has appeared in these pages, and now we know who is using it: the woman who, wanting to come face-to-face with her own desolating coldness but knowing that she will not, takes brilliant refuge in "Africa." It is her half-secret self-knowledge that enriches the narrator's speaking voice; and it is the enrichment that deepens the descriptive beauties of West with the Night. Its Africa becomes our Africa: we know why the heat is vital and the emptiness is nourishing.

Ernest Hemingway knew Beryl Markham well—she had spotted elephant for him—but West with the Night astonished him. He sang its praises everywhere. He knew the sound of a real voice when he heard it—one perhaps more real than his own—and he heard trapped in hers a

prefiguration of all the cool to come: the long literary cel-
ebration ahead of the cold within.

■   ■

At the age of fifteen I had the face of pleasure,
and yet I had no knowledge of pleasure . . . [But
that] was how everything started for me—with
that flagrant, exhausted face, those rings around
the eyes, in advance of time and experience.

Desire was Marguerite Duras's Africa: a
country, essentially unpeopled, where she lived long
enough to learn something vital about herself—more than
vital, defining.

The Lover centers on a year and a half of Marguerite
Duras's early life, and focuses on her first experience of
sexual love. It is a small, rich work of modernist narration
written by Duras at seventy, after a lifetime of devotion
both to associative prose and to the subject of desire.

The time is 1932, the place Indochina. A fifteen-and-
a-half-year-old French girl stands alone on the deck of a
ferry crossing the Mekong River from the suburb where
she lives to downtown Saigon. The river is wild and beautiful, the light a muddy glare. The girl wears a silk dress
held together with a boy's leather belt, gold-lamé high-
heeled shoes, and a man's fedora, brownish pink with a
broad black ribbon. On the deck behind her stands a limousine with a chauffeur behind the wheel. In the back of

the limo sits a Chinese man, thin and elegant, watching the girl. He gets out of the car, comes over to her, begins a conversation, trembles as he lights a cigarette, and offers to drive her wherever she is going. She agrees at once, and climbs into the car. The man will fall into an amazing passion for the girl, for her thin, white child-woman's body. The girl's absorption in her own responsiveness will become as rapt as his passion: more so. An affair begins that affects her irrevocably. It ends when she is sent to France at seventeen, in possession of the face she will bear for the rest of her life.

What the girl has learned is not only that she is a catalyst for desire but that she herself is aroused by her own powers of arousal. It's a talent: one around which to organize a life. Nasty, pleasurable thought; but, then again, so is her situation; nasty, that is, if not pleasurable.

The father, a low-grade civil servant, had come out to Indochina in the 1920s. Now he is dead and the family lives marginally, barely hanging on. The mother is drowning in depression; the younger brother is slow-witted, the elder a murderous bully. The mother loves the murderer; the narrator loves the other one. On his behalf she fights the bully. They are well matched, these two: both avid and secretive. The writing moves back and forth between the image of the girl on the ferry and that of the atmosphere at home until the reader sees that the pugnacity of will in the elder brother is equaled by the narrator's discovery in herself of this talent for desire. Equaled, and then surpassed.

She is the more ruthless by far. She listens hard when her Chinese lover tells her she will never be faithful to any man; knows that he is right; knows already that it's the power of arousal that will hold her, not any single human being. Beneath the heat that she both generates and shares in, a cold and marvelous detachment is crystallizing. Desire, she can see, is her ace in the hole: the place where she understands deeply the instrumental nature of human relations. This understanding will become her strength, her armor, her revenge, her ticket out. The year and a half with the Chinese lover is the crucible in which this knowledge is fired. That is the story Duras is wanting to tell.

How will she tell it? In a piece of narrative breakdown suitably accomplished through a speaking voice that is in itself narrative breakdown:

"Very early in my life it was too late . . . I grew old at eighteen . . .

"So, I'm fifteen and a half.

"It's on a ferry crossing the Mekong River.

"The image lasts all the way across.

"I'm fifteen and a half, there are no seasons in that part of the world, we have just the one season, hot, monotonous, we're in the long hot girdle of the earth, with no spring, no renewal."

The dominating image in the book, woven repeatedly into passage after passage, is the scene on the ferry deck. Everything important to the narrator is collected in this moment: the knowing little virgin dressed like a whore, the exotic foreigner offering sex and money, the muddy light that mirrors intent.

There she sits in Paris, Duras at seventy, leaning across the typewriter, a cigarette hanging from her lips, her eyes narrowed against smoke and distraction, staring into the picture in her mind of herself in the pink felt hat and the gold-lamé shoes, the weak, sensual lover behind her in the limousine the size of a bedroom with a glass between himself and the driver in white-cotton livery. She leans into the memory. She stares. She concentrates. What *is* it that she's looking for, trying to get straight at last?

"In the books I've written about my childhood I can't remember, suddenly, what I left out, what I said. I think I wrote about our love for our mother, but I don't know if I wrote about how we hated her too, or about our love for one another, and our terrible hatred too, in that common family history of ruin and death which was ours whatever happened, in love or in hate, and which I still can't understand however hard I try, which is still beyond my reach, hidden in the very depths of my flesh, blind as a newborn child. It's the area on whose brink silence begins. What happens there is silence, the slow travail of my whole life. I'm still there, watching those possessed children, as far away from the mystery now as I was then. I've never written, though I thought I wrote, never loved, though I thought I loved, never done anything but wait outside the closed door."

The silence in *The Lover* is overpowering, the silence among them all: the girl and her mother, the mother and her children, the brothers and the girl, the girl and the lover. The book is steeped in it. Duras is steeped in it. The space inside her for desire—the one she enters into so fully in this memoir—does not dispel the silence. On the contrary, she and the Chinese lover lie inhaling it together. It is a silence with which we are all familiar—the silence that surrounds the absence of expressive feeling; an absence that, for one and all, is unendurable, requiring sedation. With Duras, paradoxically, desire—pure, free-forming, polymorphous—remains the drug of choice:

"Hélène Lagonelle's body is . . . innocent . . . her skin's as soft as that of certain fruits . . . She makes you want to kill her . . . Those flour-white shapes, she bears them unknowingly, and offers them for hands to knead, for lips to eat . . . I'd like to eat Hélène Lagonelle's breasts as he eats mine in the room in the Chinese town where I go every night to increase my knowledge of God. I'd like to devour and be devoured by those flour-white breasts of hers.

"I am worn out with desire for Hélène Lagonelle.

"I am worn out with desire.

"I want to take Hélène Lagonelle with me to where every evening, my eyes shut, I have imparted to me the pleasure that makes you cry out. I'd like to give Hélène Lagonelle to the man who does that to me, so he may do it in turn to her. I want it to happen in my presence . . . I want her to give herself where I give myself. It's via Hélène Lagonelle's body, through it, that the ultimate pleasure would pass from him to me.

"A pleasure unto death."

Still, that terrible absence of expressive feeling—especially at home—eats at the narrator. Do what she will, there is no escaping it:

"Never a hello, a good evening, a happy New Year. Never a thank you. Never any talk. Never any need to talk. Everything always silent, distant. It's a family of stone, petrified so deeply it's impenetrable. Every day we try to kill one another, to kill. Not only do we not talk to one another, we don't even look at one another. When you're being looked at you can't look. To look is to feel curious, to be interested, to lower yourself. No one you look at is worth it. Looking is always demeaning. The word conversation is banished. I think that's what best conveys the shame and the pride. Every sort of community, whether of the family or other, is hateful to us, degrading. We're united in a fundamental shame at having to live."

Now we have arrived at the element that shapes the prose of this short, powerful memoir: Duras's unnerving endorsement of desire as a narcotic interwoven with the shame of needing human connection. Anomie, a sickness of the soul, begins in that shame. The woman who is writing this book is in mesmerized possession of that knowledge. It holds her attention at all times; never leaves her, not even for the space of a paragraph; becomes, finally, the true subject, the real protagonist of *The Lover*.

Duras worked this material for thirty years in one fictional abstraction after another. A life devoted to desire only confirmed what she had learned in the shuttered room in the Chinese quarter in Saigon in 1932—that she was alone; she was always alone; alone is what she was; and never more so than in pursuit of the pleasure unto death. But it was not until she found the narrator in herself—through the speaking voice of an amoral druggie, the one in whom anomie is a living, breathing substance—that she could say, clearly and simply, what she knew.

◾   ◾

When he was young, Wallace Stevens thought that being stuck with the will to believe in an age of unbelief left us free to feel both isolated and spontaneous: a situation he applauded. Toward the end of his life he experienced the freedom as iron in his mouth. In fact, he called it our "iron solitude." A phrase that suits to a tee the work and temperament of W. G. Sebald.

Sebald is a German in his fifties who's been living in England for the past thirty years. He writes works of nonfiction often described as unclassifiable because his narratives are endowed with a power of suggestiveness that we associate with fiction. For me, Sebald is transparently a memoirist in that his work takes its life from a speaking voice that is clearly his own and belongs to a narrator writing to puzzle out if not exactly himself, then certainly a position that will include himself in what for the sake of brevity we will call the world. *The Rings of Saturn* is a case in point.

"In August 1992," the book begins, "when the dog

days were drawing to an end, I set off to walk the county of Suffolk, in the hope of dispelling the emptiness that takes hold of me whenever I have completed a long stint of work. And in fact my hope was realized, up to a point; for I have seldom felt so carefree as I did then, walking for hours in the day through the thinly populated countryside, which stretches inland from the coast. I wonder now, however, whether there might be something in the old superstition that certain ailments of the spirit and of the body are particularly likely to beset us under the sign of the Dog Star. At all events, in retrospect I became preoccupied not only with the unaccustomed sense of freedom but also with the paralysing horror that had come over me at various times when confronted with the traces of destruction, reaching far back into the past, that were evident even in that remote place. Perhaps it was because of this that, a year to the day after I began my tour, I was taken into hospital in Norwich in a state of almost total immobility. It was then that I began in my thoughts to write these pages."

As he wanders the coast—from town to village to beach, from house to garden to park—the narrator also wanders, in long discursive passages, from one unlikely piece of association to another: the search for Thomas Browne's skull in a hospital museum; a country estate and its glamorous nineteenth-century history; the vast bombing raids of German cities during the Second World War; the wretchedness of a resort town in hopeless decline; a line of fishermen on a beach who want to be in a place "where they have the world behind them, and before them nothing but emptiness"; the natural history of the herring; an extensive memory of a hotel lobby in The Hague; the story of Roger Casement folding into that of Joseph Conrad; an eccentric gentleman's even more eccentric will; a narrow-gauge railway on a river bridge leading into a long disquisition on nineteenth-century China; the Croatian massacre of Bosnians in the 1940s; a medieval church tower on a beach, the memory of which once drew poets like Swinburne to the long-gone seaside town of Dunwich.

On and on *The Rings of Saturn* goes, accumulating through a stack of very simple sentences a seamless tapestry of association, elaborate and far-reaching, that slowly begins to seem of a piece, although the reader is hard put to know why. No matter how we turn these associations over in our minds, taken all together, as agents of a unifying idea, they do not yield an intelligent pattern. Finally, we realize that it is the narrator who is the "agent": he himself is the unifying idea. Not through what he tells us about himself or even through what he sees as he travels, but through the *way* he sees what he sees. It is the character of the persona's perspective that provides the narrative its striking inner life.

In scene after scene after scene, it now dawns on us, the most ordinary of prospects—a beachfront, a village street, a hotel lobby—makes the narrator observe that he feels himself standing at the edge of time; at the start of eternity; at the outermost limits of the beginning—or the end; with the world always at his back, emptiness perpetually before him. Then the reader realizes how many times the world has been described as "leaden-colored." Repeatedly we are told that the sea, the sky, the day is leaden-colored. And then how often we hear the phrase "hardly a living soul was to be seen." On a village or a town street, in an estate park or garden, on an expanse of beach or a landscaped something-or-other: hardly a living soul is ever to be seen. Casually these observations are inserted. Here or there. In a word, a sentence, a fragment. At what turns out to be just the right moment in just the right paragraph. The one that resembles a stone dropping straight to the subliminal bottom.

Every description of the visible world; every association past, present, future; every bit of memory, conjecture, or speculation implies a state of being destitute of human connection. On a small propeller plane that services the route from Amsterdam to Norwich the point is suddenly driven home:

"Spread out beneath us lay one of the most densely-populated regions in Europe, with endless terraces, sprawling satellite towns, business parks and shining glass houses which looked like large quadrangular ice floes drifting across this corner of the continent where not a patch is left to its own devices. Over the centuries the land had been regulated, cultivated and built on until the whole region was transformed into a geometrical pattern . . . Nowhere, however, was a single human being to be seen. No matter whether one is flying over Newfoundland or the sea of lights that stretches from Boston to Philadelphia after nightfall, over the Arabian deserts which gleam like mother-of-pearl, over the Ruhr or the city of Frankfurt. It is as though there were no people, only the things they have made and in which they are hiding. One sees the places where they live and the roads that link them, one sees the smoke rising from their houses and factories, one sees the vehicles in which they sit, but one sees not the people themselves."

It is the word "hiding" that does it. A walking tour in a country famous for its domestication of walking tours becomes a futurist movie, foretold from the very beginning, we now recall, when the narrator tells us he traveled down to the coast in an old diesel train car where people "sat in the half-light on the threadbare seats, all of them facing the engine and as far away from each other as they could be, and so silent, that not a word might have passed their lips in the whole of their lives."

Clearly, the bleakness originates from within. It is the material condition of the narrator's inner life, the walls that contain him, the prison of his own personality. It is from inside this prison that he is speaking.

Yet the hedged-in partialness of view yields a brilliant creation because of the depth, and the spirit, with which Sebald enters into his own inner condition, the expansiveness with which he occupies and inhabits it. In this sense he reminds us of Beckett, who made rich, lasting poetry out of his own dark night of the soul also by entering into it so remarkably, and applying what he found there so persuasively, that readers and theatergoers came away exhilarated by the bleakness, alive to their own experience and to the singularity of their moment. So it is with Sebald.

The human absence in *The Rings of Saturn* does not feel bad or painful or sinister. It feels, in fact, quite natural, as though it is being experienced by a man in his element, one for whom the solitary wander has long been the only reality. The calm of Sebald's solitariness is immense—as large as Loren Eiseley's universe—the calm and the silence. The narrator is neither repelled by this silence nor does he embrace it. He simply rests in it: concentrates on it: without shock, resentment, or the need for sedation. Rather like a Trappist monk who might also have the power to move into and then beyond anomie, thereby rediscovering the world.

Sebald associates so fully, so freely, so unstintingly—to the sight of an empty coastline, a decayed resort, the tale of one historic massacre after another—that the reporting itself becomes a kind of poetry, the bleakness within a counterpoint to the enormity and wonder of endless world making. We come, through this wide-angle, freewheeling inner associativeness pouring out of a man who will end up hospitalized for depression, to feel the immensity of human existence: not its smallness or meanness or pointlessness. In the act of responding so prodigiously to what he sees, recalls, and broods upon, this calm, solitary, pilgrim-like narrator performs a peculiar act of compassion toward world-and-self, one that extends a lifeline of hope.

In a hotel lobby in Holland, Sebald remembers a visit he has recently made to the grave of his patron saint in Nuremberg, "of whom legend has it that he was the son of a king, from Dacia or Denmark, who married a French princess in Paris. During the wedding night, the story goes, he was afflicted with a sense of profound unworthiness. Today, he is supposed to have said to his bride, our bodies are adorned, but tomorrow they will be food for worms. Before the break of day, he fled, making a pilgrimage to Italy, where he lived in solitude until he felt the power to work miracles arising within him . . . [and] went over the Alps to Germany. At Regensburg he crossed the Danube on his cloak, and there made a broken glass whole again; and, in the house of a wheelwright too mean to spare the kindling, lit a fire with icicles. This story of the burning of the frozen substance of life has, of late, meant much to me, and I wonder now whether inner coldness and desolation may not be the pre-condition for making the world believe, by a kind of fraudulent showmanship, that one's own wretched heart is still aglow."

And there you have it. The allure of *The Rings of Saturn*. Its strange beauty. An account of human solitude—wide, deep, ever present—is being given us now, at this moment in our spiritually depleted history, by a narrator who needs to believe that his wretched heart is still aglow.

It is, I think, a measure of the bankruptcy of fiction that *The Rings of Saturn* is repeatedly called a novel. Sebald is doing an old-fashioned thing here, entering into the narrating self in a way that ignores modernism and postmodernism alike and is as far from the gargantuan, language-besotted, mythical abstractions of contemporary fiction writers like Pynchon, Powers, and DeLillo as literature will allow itself to go. Yet the critics cannot believe that the power to make us feel this, our one and only life, as very few novels actually do these days, is coming from a memoirist—a nonfiction truth speaker—who has entered our common situation and is telling the story we now want told. But it is.

CONCLUSION

This book grew out of fifteen years of teaching in M.F.A. programs, where I have learned that you cannot teach people how to write—the gift of dramatic expressiveness, of a natural sense of structure, of making language sink down beneath the surface of description, all that is inborn, cannot be taught—but you can teach people how to read, how to develop judgment about a piece of writing: their own as well as that of others. You can teach them how to puzzle out the experience buried in a mass of material and to see whether it is being shaped on the page; how to search out the link between a narrative line and the wisdom that compels it; how to ask, Who is speaking, what is being said, and what is the relation between the two? All this you can teach if it is your predilection so to teach. I discovered that it was mine.

From the moment I found myself standing in front of a memoir-writing class with a hunk of manuscript in my hand, asking, What is this all about?—and the answer came back, It's about this dysfunctional family in Cincinnati, and I said, No, no. What is it *about*?—I saw that my classes would be reading as *I* needed to read: looking for the inner context that makes a piece of writing larger than its immediate circumstance; *places* a writer's thought and feeling; imposes shape and reveals inner purpose; the thing that is invariably being addressed when one says to *any* writer of imagination, But what is it about? and does not expect to hear, It's about this family in Cincinnati.

From the first I thought that to teach writing was to teach my students how to keep on reading until we all saw as clearly as we could what was driving the writer. What, we would ask of the manuscript, was the larger preoccupation here? the true experience? the real subject? Not that such questions could be answered, only that it seemed vital to me that they be asked. To approach the work in hand as any ordinary reader might was to learn not *how* to write but—more important by far—*why* one was writing. In these classes both I and my students discovered repeatedly that this was more than half the battle.

A student once brought to class a piece about the grandfather she had never known. The piece began, "I followed my grandmother up the narrow, crumbling steps to the attic of her house in a tiny midwestern town that not so long ago had been farmland. The day was cold and down in the street below children called to one another through the raw wind. My grandmother's legs were swollen and heavily veined; her walk leaden, her body held tightly inside the housedress she perpetually wore. My grandfather had built this house forty years before and then one fine day he went out for cigarettes and never came back. All that remained of him—letters, clothes, pictures—was locked in a trunk in the attic."

Paragraph upon paragraph followed in the same cluttered, errant fashion, the pages mounting up but failing to accumulate, falling repeatedly into abstract ruminations on memory, shadows, dreams. In class we struggled to make sense of the piece, reading it as a whole again and again, trying hard to understand wherein lay its failure to cohere. At last someone said, "It's not about the grandfather; it's about the grandmother." A lightbulb went on in the room. And in the writer. The following week the opening paragraph read:

"I followed my grandmother up the narrow, crumbling steps to the attic where my runaway grandfather was, so to speak, stored. Her swollen legs were heavy, slow, reluctant. Every inch of her tight, hard body exuded the characteristic belligerence she dared not express openly. She was, after all, the 'nicest' of nice midwesterners; the kind whose narrow mouth never uttered a negative. She had lived in this house as a deserted wife and mother for thirty-five years, never once mentioning the man who'd walked out one day never to return, leaving her behind in the hardscrabble farm town he'd brought her to. My mother, her daughter, hardly ever came back, although she sent me regularly for a few weeks in summer. I had always felt that I wasn't wanted at home; to be deposited here on these gloomy visits with my tight-lipped grandmother was all the proof I needed. But now, for the first time (I was fourteen) I had asked to 'see' Grandpa, and to my surprise she had assented."

Clearly, the piece was on its way. It was simply the repeated act of asking, What is this all about? that had led the writer to the point of view that had released the narrator and focused the subject struggling to emerge from inchoate material.

The discussion in my class, I soon discovered, seemed to preclude the question of craft and put me down on the other side of an emphasis prevalent in the workshop game—craft being the bread and butter of M.F.A. programs—one that I find appalling, as the concentration on skills is, I think, the bane of contemporary literature's existence. An excellent little book about classic prose style, *Clear and Simple as the Truth*, puts the case for me admirably when it observes that although "writing must lead to skills, and . . . skills visibly mark the performance, the activity does not come from the skills, nor does it consist of using them. In this way, writing is like conversation . . . A bad conversationalist may have a very high level of verbal skills but perform poorly because he does not conceive of conversation as distinct from monologue. No further cultivation of verbal skill will remedy his problem. Conversely, a very good conversationalist may have inferior verbal skills, but a firm grasp on [the] concepts [of] reciprocity and turn-taking that lie at the heart of the activity. Neither conversation nor writing can be learned merely by acquiring verbal skills, and any attempt to teach writing by teaching writing skills detached from underlying conceptual issues is doomed."

Any attempt to teach writing, *Clear and Simple as the Truth* might have added, out of anything other than that which the teacher knows intimately rather than theoretically is also doomed. Theories of creative writing I find even more damaging than questions of craft. It seems to me that as teachers of writing, we are there only to make the widest and most thoughtful sense of our own experience. Out of that alone comes useful extrapolation.

It was as a teacher of writing that I discovered that to know "who is speaking, what is being said, and what is the relation between the two" had become my single-minded practice—these were years in which I, the teacher, was teaching myself how to read what I, the writer, was soon to write. The single-mindedness proved a strength, a limitation, and a source of revelation. This way of grouping one's thought around the reading of a manuscript was, I knew, only one of many—a hundred *other* vital perspectives, for a hundred other teachers to light on, would do just as well—but for me "Get the narrator, and you've got the piece" proved an irresistible guide to how essays and memoirs organize a mass of raw material. This was the perspective that, in my hands, yielded breadth of interpretation. The experience taught me something crucial about how we read.

Writing enters into us when it gives us information about ourselves we are in need of *at the time that we are reading*. How obvious the thought seems once it has been articulated! As with love, politics, or friendship: readiness is all. When a book of merit is trashed upon publication, or one of passing value praised to the skies, it is not that the book, in either case, is being read by the wrong or the right people, it is that the wrong or the right moment is being intersected with. *This* book, good or great though it may be, sinks like a stone because what it has to say cannot be taken in at the moment; while *that* book, transparently ephemeral, is well received because what *it* is addressing is alive—now, right now—in the shared psyche. Which is perhaps as it should be. The inner life is nourished only if it gets what it needs when it needs it.

In looking over what I have written, I am struck by the intense partialness of the undertaking, reflected both in what I have read and in how I have read. I find myself remembering all the people who, all along the way, as I confided one memoir or essay enthusiasm after another, repeatedly called to my attention not only the different kinds of essays and memoirs I was ignoring but all that was not being addressed in what I *was* reading. True, I readily agreed each time, all too true—as though to adopt an undefensive posture was to mitigate the charge—but secretly I think I believed that if I let a ribbon of selective association unfold, unimpeded, an inner coherence would prevail that would result in: all things considered. I was wrong. The limit of my concern is apparent. How does the writer of personal narrative pull from his or her own boring, agitated self the truth speaker who will tell the story that needs to be told? That is the question I asked, and in the course of answering, I trained my eyes on the writing: how it got done, how it functioned, took its place in the world, helped alter literary history. To read out of one's own narrow but clarified need, I concluded, was to teach oneself better how to write—and how to teach writing.

A GUIDE FOR
WRITERS, TEACHERS,
AND STUDENTS

The discussion questions, exercises, and suggested reading list that follow were prepared by the publisher to help readers focus their reading of Vivian Gornick's *The Situation and the Story*, an incisive exploration of how the personal narrative achieves its power. We hope these will offer a deeper understanding of Gornick's analysis and suggest ways in which others might apply her approaches to their own writing.

QUESTIONS FOR DISCUSSION

1. In discussing her own first book, a personal account of her experiences in Egypt, Gornick says that she eventually realized that the problem with her writing was that

she lacked detachment, had failed even to understand that detachment was necessary, that "without detachment there can be no story" (p. 12). Why is detachment especially important in *personal* narrative? What limitations arise when the writer is too close to her material?

2. Gornick claims that "every work of literature has both a situation and a story. The situation is the context or circumstance, sometimes the plot; the story is the emotional experience that preoccupies the writer: the insight, the wisdom, the thing one has come to say" (p. 13). What is the situation of *The Situation and the Story*? What is its context or circumstance? What is its central insight, the thing Gornick "has come to say"?

3. What qualities does Gornick admire in Joan Didion's "In Bed," Harry Crews's "Why I Live Where I Live," and Edward Hoagland's "The Courage of Turtles" (pp. 36–52)? What trajectories do these essays follow? What do their narrators discover and reveal about themselves in the act of writing?

4. Gornick begins the chapter on memoir by pointing out: "Thirty years ago people who thought they had a story to tell sat down to write a novel. Today they sit down to write a memoir" (p. 89). How does she explain this shift? Do you agree? What other reasons might account for the recent popularity of memoir and other forms of autobiographical writing?

5. Gornick writes that nonfiction "builds only when the narrator is involved not in confession but in this kind of self-investigation, the kind that means to provide motion, purpose, and dramatic tension" (p. 35). What is the difference between confession and self-investigation? How is that difference reflected in the examples Gornick cites by Beryl Markham and Marguerite Duras?

6. Embedded in *The Situation and the Story* is an ongoing argument against modernism, or against what modernism and postmodernism have done to narrative writing. In discussing W. G. Sebald's memoir, *The Rings of Saturn*, Gornick says: "It is, I think, a measure of the bankruptcy of fiction that *The Rings of Saturn* is repeatedly called a novel" (p. 155). Why is Gornick disillusioned with modernist narrative strategies and the fiction that results from them? What satisfactions does she feel more traditional narratives offer? How do her examples, of Sebald and others, support her position?

7. In her conclusion, Gornick says that after fifteen years of teaching in M.F.A. programs, she has learned that "you cannot teach people how to write" (p. 159). And yet her book is both insightful and instructive. What can be learned about how to write from *The Situation and the Story*? What precepts can you apply to your own writing? What passages and examples seem most relevant to your own writing process?

EXERCISES AND PRACTICAL APPLICATIONS

1. Gornick praises James Baldwin and George Orwell for interweaving the personal and the political, for exhibiting "a rare depth of inquiry into the self" (p. 85), and for having the courage to include themselves in the dehumanizing effects of racism that both writers observe in the world around them. Write a personal essay on a political subject about which you feel strongly and in which you are somehow implicated.

2. In discussing Loren Eiseley's memoir *All the Strange Hours*, Gornick concludes: "If the solitude of the self is the real subject, memoirists generally do better when they speak through the filter of that which passes for a subject well beyond themselves" (p. 136). Write a brief personal narrative in which you approach some aspect of yourself by writing about a subject beyond yourself.

3. Read a memoir or personal essay and write a critique employing some of the principles that Gornick develops in *The Situation and the Story*. Is the narrator sufficiently detached? Trustworthy? Does the writer have a central insight that structures the story? Does the writing possess a depth of inquiry that engages a disinterested reader?

4. Much of *The Situation and the Story* is concerned with writing as self-discovery, or with the relation between *who* is speaking and *what* is being said. Write a short

personal narrative about a moment of important self-insight or self-definition, a moment when you made a breakthrough in discovering or becoming who you are. Try to develop a narrative voice that both speaks about and embodies that insight.

5. In discussing the essays on marriage by Lynn Darling and Natalia Ginzburg, Gornick observes that "each writer is discovering the mysterious in the familiar" (pp. 74–75). Write a brief personal essay about a familiar subject, marriage if appropriate, that attempts to reveal the mystery at the heart of the ordinary.

6. "What happened to the writer," Gornick argues, "is not what matters; what matters is the large sense the writer is able to *make* of what happened" (p. 91). Write about a small but important experience in your life and try to make that large sense of it that Gornick feels is required of strong nonfiction writing.

7. Revisit a piece of personal writing that you worked on before reading *The Situation and the Story* and revise it with Gornick's insights and perspectives in mind.

SUGGESTIONS FOR
FURTHER READING

Judith Barrington, *Writing the Memoir: From Truth to Art*; Annie Dillard and Cort Conley, eds., *Modern American Memoirs*; Patricia Hampl, *I Could Tell You Stories:*

Sojourns in the Land of Memory; Anne Lamott, *Bird by Bird: Some Instructions on Writing and Life*; Phillip Lopate, ed., *The Art of the Personal Essay*; Jane Taylor McDonnell, *Living to Tell the Tale: A Guide to Writing Memoir*; and William Zinsser, ed., *Inventing the Truth: The Art and Craft of Memoir*.